220
Green Book

TIMEF[

CW00734553

HORSES TO ᖴOLLOW

2021/22 JUMPS SEASON

CONTENTS

TIMEF⊙RM

ISBN 978-1-8380349-2-4 Price £10.95

Printed and bound by
Charlesworth Press,
Wakefield, UK 01924 204830

SECTION

Timeform's Fifty To Follow, carefully chosen by members of Timeform's editorial staff, are listed below with their respective page numbers. A selection of ten (**marked in bold with a** ★) is made for those who prefer a smaller list.

The form summary for each horse is shown after its age, colour, sex and pedigree. The summary shows the distance, the state of the going and where the horse finished in each of its races since the start of the 2020/21 season. Performances are in chronological sequence with the date of its last race shown at the end (F–ran on Flat).

The distance of each race is given in furlongs. Steeplechase form figures are prefixed by the letter 'c', hurdle form figures by the letter 'h' and NH Flat race or bumper form figures by the letter 'b'.

The going is symbolised as follows: f–firm, m–good to firm; g–good, d–good to soft; s–soft; v–heavy.

Placings are indicated, up to the sixth place, by use of superior figures, an asterisk being used to denote a win and superior letters are used to convey what happened to a horse during the race: F–fell, pu–pulled up, ur–unseated rider, bd–brought down, su–slipped up, ro–ran out.

The Timeform Rating of a horse is simply the merit of the horse expressed in pounds and is arrived at by careful examination of its running against other horses. The ratings range from 175+ for the champions down to a figure of around 55 for selling platers. Symbols attached to the ratings: 'p'–likely to improve; 'P'–capable of much better form; '+'–the horse may be better than we have rated it.

Bali Body (Ire)   h116

6 b.g. Doyen(Ire) – Burnt Oil Babe (Ire) (Beneficial)
2020/21 h22v⁶ h21v⁵ h26v* h25g² Apr 3

Foxtrot Racing and Dr Richard Newland have struck up a formidable partnership over the years and they have an interesting prospect for novice handicap chases on their hands in Bali Body.

Bali Body was a work in progress last term, making his first start under Rules in a novice hurdle at Fontwell in January. He offered something to work on when finishing sixth behind Beauport on that occasion and his season was one of gentle progression from there. Fifth in a similar contest at Warwick in February, he was then stepped up in trip to get off the mark at Hereford the following month, overcoming a mistake at the third last to win comfortably by two and a quarter lengths.

All three of Bali Body's runs up to that point had been on heavy ground, but he showed he can handle a quicker surface on his final start at Carlisle in April. Making his handicap debut from a BHA mark of 118, he beat all bar Storm Nelson, who was thriving and well-in under a penalty, ultimately passing the post 11 lengths behind that rival.

Bali Body has been dropped slightly in the weights for the new campaign and a switch to long distance novice handicap chases surely awaits. He was second on his sole outing in Irish points and looks just the sort his shrewd handler will get on a roll with at some stage. Everything about him suggests that he will stay beyond 3m and there's a good programme there for connections to exploit. **Dr Richard Newland**

Conclusion: *Improved with racing over hurdles in 2020/21 and should progress further granted a stiffer stamina test over fences; BHA mark of 117 also looks workable*

Bear Ghylls (Ire)   h145+
6 br.g. Arcadio (Ger) – Inch Princess (Ire) (Oscar (Ire))
2020/21 h20d* h16v* h18v* h21d⁴ Mar 17

Not to be confused with intrepid adventurer and TV regular Bear Grylls, this son of Arcadio is likely to feature on many a horse to follow list this season. And with good reason.

A €22,000-purchase as a three-year-old, Bear Ghylls sprang a 33/1 surprise in a Warwick bumper on his only start of the 2019/20 campaign. There was no hint of a fluke about that performance as he travelled strongly throughout before powering clear from the home turn, ultimately winning by 19 lengths to earn himself a spot in last year's *Fifty* as a smart prospect for novice hurdling. Bear Ghylls duly lived up to that billing—and more—during the latest season. His hurdling bow came at Lingfield in October and a blunder at the last was his only scare. He recovered quickly to win by four and a half lengths from Make Me A Believer, who went on to finish third, beaten just half a length behind Adrimel, in the Leamington Novices' Hurdle at Warwick. Bear Ghylls showed that he too was ready to have his sights raised when winning his next two starts, justifying very short odds at Ffos Las in November before taking his record to four from four on handicap debut at Exeter in January. In control when hitting the last at Exeter, he proceeded to cruise clear on the run-in to defy an opening BHA mark of 130 by five lengths with a bit in hand.

Bear Ghylls was stepped up markedly in grade after that for the Ballymore Novices' Hurdle at the Cheltenham Festival, where he lost his unbeaten record but still showed improved form to pass the post around 12 lengths behind Bob Olinger in fourth. He might well have done even better had he jumped more fluently, making several mistakes on the way round, and his strength at the finish was particularly praiseworthy given that he raced freely throughout.

On looks and demeanour, Bear Ghylls is every inch a chaser and seems sure to take high rank in the novice chasing ranks in 2021/22. He's yet to race beyond 21f but appeals as the sort to stay further and must be considered an exciting prospect. He can run up a sequence before the bigger tests of the spring loom large. **Nicky Martin**

Conclusion: *Lengthy gelding who ran well up considerably in class when losing his unbeaten record at Cheltenham; will make a chaser and should progress and win races in the novice ranks*

Boothill (Ire) h128P

6 b. or br.g. Presenting – Oyster Pipit (Ire) (Accordion)
2020/21 h16s* Dec 10

Here's a most exciting prospect for the coming season. Boothill has been restricted to just two starts in his first two seasons under Rules but, such is the impression he's made in winning a bumper at Kempton and a novice hurdle at Taunton, he's one we have to keep on the right side.

The form of Boothill's bumper victory (in a good time) was already working out well by the time he rolled into Somerset in December for his debut over timber. And he didn't disappoint. A fine physical specimen, he oozed class in everything he did at Taunton. Not fluent at the first, he hurdled efficiently afterwards and was always racing on the bridle. In front turning in, he quickened clear in a matter of strides to win by nine and a half lengths in a race which is proving strong form, with four of the next five home going on to win races subsequently.

Unfortunately, Boothill himself wasn't seen again during the latest season due to a niggling problem with a splint, but he is reported to have made a full recovery and remains firmly in the "could be anything" category heading into the 2021/22 campaign. He is open to significant improvement over hurdles but also has the option of going novice chasing, which seems to be the preferred route.

A well-made gelding who filled the runner-up spot on both his starts in Irish points, Boothill looks to possess all the necessary tools to take well to fences and, hopefully, he'll get a clear run this time to show exactly what he is capable of. He's looked something a bit special on the limited evidence we have so far and will be one to look out for in novice chases at around 2m. *Harry Fry*

Conclusion: *Unbeaten in two starts under Rules and the feeling remains that we've only scratched the surface of his ability; looks a potential top-notcher with a view to novice chasing*

Bravemansgame (Fr) h146

6 b.g. Brave Mansonnien (Fr) - Genifique (Fr) (Nickname (Fr))
2020/21 h16g2 h17d* h21g* h21d* h21d3 h25d2 Apr 9

"Denman won the Challow. He is the same sort of big, scopey horse that will make a chaser. This one has probably got a little more boot than Denman had. He is a hard horse to follow, but he is going the right way. He has got it all."

A significant comment from Paul Nicholls shortly after Bravemansgame became his latest winner of the Challow Novices' Hurdle at Newbury in December. And, while the six-year-old came up short at the major spring festivals, the rich promise remains.

Bravemansgame is every inch a chaser on looks

Bravemansgame began his hurdling career by chasing home subsequent Betfair Hurdle winner Soaring Glory over 2m at Chepstow. It was then to Exeter in November for an impressive defeat of Runswick Bay before a similarly dominant success over 2½m at Newbury later that month. That teed him up for the Challow, run over the same course and distance, where he was in front after a hurdle and made the rest to beat Star Gate by an emphatic 10 lengths.

That victory in Berkshire marked Bravemansgame out as the chief home hope to repel the Irish armada in the novice hurdling ranks at Cheltenham. The Ballymore Novices' Hurdle was the chosen March target and he duly ran well but simply found a speedier model in the shape of Bob Olinger too good. Bravemansgame finished third, with Gaillard du Mesnil taking the forecast spot, before stepping up to 3m for the Sefton Novices' Hurdle at Aintree. Sent off the 13/8 favourite at Aintree, Bravemansgame had no problem with the trip and just seemed to bump into a better one on the day, namely 66/1 chance Ahoy Senor, who made all to win by seven lengths in ready fashion.

Bravemansgame's season may have stalled a little after the Challow, but it still represented a fine first one over timber, with the promise of much more to come as a chaser. That journey will begin shortly and, while the Denman-comparison will be a tough one to shake-off, it will be a surprise if Bravemansgame isn't a big player in all the major staying novice prizes. **Paul Nicholls**

Conclusion: *Irish point winner who showed smart form in six starts over hurdles and will surely raise his game as novice chaser; looks a leading contender for Grade 1 honours at around 3m*

Calico (Ger) h140

5 b.g. Soldier Hollow - Casanga (Ire) (Rainbow Quest (USA))
2020/21 h16v* h16g² h16s* h16g⁴ Apr 18

Named after a plain-woven textile used for bags in banks and financial institutions, the expectation is that Calico can prove a real money-spinner for the Skelton team in valuable handicap hurdles.

A useful performer on the Flat—he was fourth in the 2020 German St Leger—Calico won two of his four races over timber during the latest season with the promise of more to come. He isn't straightforward, we saw that on his second start in the Sky Bet Dovecote Novices' Hurdle at Kempton, but in terms of raw ability his shrewd team have plenty to work on.

Calico's jumping career started with a smooth win in the Ludlow mud in January, impressing with not only how he went through the race but his fluent hurdling too. He was then sent to Kempton for the Dovecote and for much of the contest he looked like taking the step up in class in his stride. He again raced on the bridle and loomed up three out looking all over the winner. However, he made a mistake at the next flight and was far from fluent at the last either. Calico should still have won but wandered around on the run-in, allowing Cape Gentlemen an unexpected second invitation to snatch the prize, one he took with relish.

Calico was clearly still raw and a confidence-booster back in novice company at Warwick, when a smooth winner as the 4/1-on favourite, teed him up for a tilt at the Scottish Champion Hurdle at Ayr. He wasn't disgraced when making his handicap debut from a BHA mark of 139 on the last occasion, but his lack of experience told in the end, looking a danger to all when pecking on landing three out before a mistake at the last finally ended his chance. He finished fourth, beaten just over 10 lengths behind the winner Milkwood, and gained valuable experience which should stand him in good stead in the coming months.

Calico starts his second season over hurdles on the same mark and open to further progress. He is certainly in the right hands to go on improving and appeals as just the sort to thrive granted a strong gallop in a big-field handicap scenario, with a race such as the Betfair Hurdle at Newbury likely to feature on his agenda. **Dan Skelton**

Conclusion: *Strong-travelling sort who looked a work in progress during his first season over timber; likely to progress further and make an impact in the big handicap hurdles at around 2m*

Code Name Lise (Ire) b95

5 b.m. Fame And Glory - Firth of Five (Ire) (Flemensfirth (USA))
2020/21 F16v² F16s* F16v Mar 13

Owner Emma Banks has already enjoyed a glorious racing year in 2021 thanks to the exploits of Lady Bowthorpe. And now the music agent to the likes of Kyle Minogue and Katie Perry has a young hurdler to go to war with too through the winter.

Code Name Lise is named after Larry Loftis' acclaimed book which tells the true story of Odette Sansom, the British spy who operated in occupied France and fell in love with her commanding officer during World War II. It's a remarkable story and, while the equine version's own tale is only in its infancy, the best chapters lie ahead. The journey will start in the coming months where she can be expected to take high rank in novice hurdles against her own sex.

Code Name Lise had three starts last season in bumpers and each offered encouragement. She made her debut at Warwick in January where she travelled powerfully and, after being short of room on the turn in, kept on well to finish second behind Gold Bullion. She was then switched to a race confined to her own sex at Ascot and, having impressed in the parade ring beforehand, delivered a taking performance on the track. Again, the feature was how she went through the race but this time she was in front a furlong out and merely pushed out to beat Miss Fairfax by a length and a quarter.

It was no surprise when all roads then led to the listed mares' bumper on Imperial Cup day at Sandown. Bryony Frost was in the saddle and her partner again went well—too well at times—through the race. She looked a danger to all two out only for her run to flatten out in the bottomless ground. Physically, Code Name Lise is the sort to progress with another summer on her back and she appeals as one who can run up a sequence over timber before her sights are raised again. ***Lucy Wadham***

Conclusion: *Lots of promise in bumpers during the latest season and appeals as the sort to make up into a useful novice hurdler in 2021/22*

Come On Teddy (Ire) h134

7 b.g. Fame And Glory – Theatre View (Ire) (Old Vic)
2020/21 h23v⁴ h24s* h25v³ h24d³ h25d⁶ Apr 10

There were 23 Irish-trained winners at the 2021 Cheltenham Festival. I'm sure you're aware of the fact it was a record and the ramifications are still ongoing. At the time of writing there's talk of a revamp to the British programme to encourage more competition, an equivalent of the Dublin Racing Festival. Either way, it's going to take time to restore the balance of power and the home contingent can surely expect more short-term pain given the strength of the Irish in the novice ranks, over both hurdles and fences, during the latest season. It wasn't restricted to the novices, either, with each of the five handicap hurdles at the meeting going the way of Irish-trained runners, including a five-length victory for Mrs Milner in the Pertemps Final.

A little further back in third in the Pertemps Final was Come On Teddy, who was the only member of the home team to finish in the first four and could go close again if continuing to go the right way this season. Shaping as if in need of the run on his reappearance at Uttoxeter in November, Come On Teddy improved to win with a bit in hand at Cheltenham three weeks later. It was clear the Pertemps would be the target from there and he duly took in a qualifier at Warwick in January, finishing third behind the impressive Imperial Alcazar. Come On Teddy comprehensively reversed that form at the Festival the following month, coming from the rear of the field with a strong late run which carried him into the placings, even appearing to finish with running left.

Come On Teddy was unsuited by the way things developed on his final outing at Aintree, but he starts the new campaign on a BHA mark of 137, only 3 lb higher than when placed at Cheltenham. It will be no surprise if all roads lead back to the Pertemps and, while the Irish armada will again be strong, there is likely to be at least one live home threat awaiting them at Prestbury Park. ***Tom George***

Conclusion: *Progressive staying handicap hurdler who ran well in the Pertemps Final at Cheltenham; likely to go on improving, especially when stamina is at a premium*

Come On Teddy (white cap) is the type to go on improving over hurdles

Craigneiche (Ire) h139p

7 br.g. Flemensfirth (USA) – Itsalark (Ire) (Definite Article)
2020/21 h19s* h21d² Mar 17

We only saw Craigneiche twice during the latest season, but both those runs were full of promise and there is no doubting his potential if he stands more regular racing for his top yard in 2021/22.

Craigneiche broke a blood vessel when winning a novice hurdle at Doncaster in January 2020 and then spent a full calendar year on the sidelines before returning to action at Ascot. Stablemate Janika was stronger in the betting at Ascot and that was little surprise given Craigneiche's behaviour in the preliminaries (sweating and very much on his toes). In the race itself, however, Craigneiche belied his absence and market weakness in good style, proving himself some way ahead of an opening BHA mark of 127. He was briefly outpaced approaching the straight but hung in there and rallied to lead on landing two out, forging clear from there to beat Arrivederci by seven lengths.

The Coral Cup at the Cheltenham Festival was next on the cards for Craigneiche who lined up from a 12 lb higher mark than when successful at Ascot. He was much calmer in the preliminaries in a red hood and, though unable to follow up, there was still plenty to like about his effort as he fared best of the home contingent behind Heaven Help Us, who stole a march at the start. Craigneiche wasn't fluent at the third last and was bumped on the home turn but he ran on strongly.

Craigneiche kicks off the 2021/22 campaign on a BHA mark of 142 and remains relatively unexposed, appealing as just the sort of lightly raced, progressive hurdler his yard does so well with. Crucially, the way Craigneiche came home at Cheltenham suggests he will be suited by a step up to 3m at some stage, too, and he will be firmly on the radar for a big handicap at around that trip in the coming months. ***Nicky Henderson***

Conclusion: *Lightly raced sort who ran a huge race in the Coral Cup and looks handicapped to win a big pot when stepped up to 3m+ in 2021/22*

Demachine (Ire) c145

7 b.g. Flemensfirth (USA) – Dancingonthemoon (Ire) (Milan)
2020/21 c22d* c24d* c22d³ c24s² Feb 20

Considering he's closely related to Sub Lieutenant and from the family of Lord Windermere, it's little surprise that Demachine has already made up into a better chaser than hurdler—and he hasn't finished yet by our reckoning.

Trainer Kerry Lee wasted little time in switching Demachine to the larger obstacles in 2020/21, starting him out in a novice handicap at Uttoxeter in October. He immediately proved himself better than a BHA mark of 122, going strongly through the race and readily picking off the trailblazing Midnight Vicar approaching the final fence. The handicapper was quick to act, but even a 10 lb hike in the weights couldn't prevent Demachine from following up at Ascot in November. He once again jumped fluently and quickly asserted from the last to beat Young Bull, third behind him at Uttoxeter, by three and three quarter lengths despite being 9 lb worse off at weights with that rival.

Demachine failed to add to his tally in two subsequent starts, but there was plenty to like about both efforts. He was a little keen and found Paint The Clouds too hot to handle from an 8 lb higher mark at Newbury in December, losing second in the dying strides to Dickie Diver. Connections then opted to roll the dice in the Reynoldstown Novices' Chase at Ascot as he reappeared after eight weeks off and a breathing operation. Demachine looked a big threat to the freewheeling Remastered—another member of the *Fifty*— early in the straight at Ascot, but he was outstayed by that rival on the run-in with the pair pulling nearly 30 lengths clear of the only other finisher, Kalooki, who went on to be touched off in a handicap from a BHA mark of 142 on his next start.

Demachine has only had four starts over fences and his profile is a positive one. His best days are almost certainly ahead of him and he starts his second season over fences on a BHA mark of 142. That looks more than fair judged on the balance of his form and, with plenty of good prizes to aim at, he's one to have on your side in the big handicap chases at up to 3m. ***Kerry Lee***

Conclusion: *Progressive in his first season over fences and may yet have more to offer; looks well up to winning a big handicap from a BHA mark of 142*

 # Do Your Job (Ire) h139
7 b.g. Fame And Glory – Full of Birds (Fr) (Epervier Bleu)
2020/21 h16v* h16v* h16s² h16s⁴ h18d² h16d² Apr 9

Michael Scudamore is perhaps best known for winning the 2013 Welsh Grand National with Monbeg Dude, after whom one of the trainer's three yards at his picturesque Eccleswall Court facility is currently named. Scudamore has enjoyed other moments in the spotlight since the 'Dude' delivered at Chepstow under a super-cool Paul Carberry ride, though. Next Sensation's Grand Annual success at the 2015 Cheltenham Festival, which resonated on several levels having been ridden by older brother Tom, stands out amongst them, while Nada To Prada also gave the yard a notable victory when successful at listed level in the Haydock mud in December.

Another horse to represent Scudamore with distinction during the latest season was Do Your Job, who came close to providing his trainer with a first Grade 1 success when second in the Top Novices' Hurdle at Aintree in April. Though sent off 12/1, running so well in top-class company in the spring was hardly a shock to most onlookers, Scudamore having gone on record earlier in the campaign to suggest he felt Do Your Job may end up being the best horse he's ever trained.

Those claims were looking rosy after Do Your Job won novice hurdles at Ffos Las and Ayr, both in October, before slightly lesser displays at Haydock and Sandown prompted a breathing operation. The minor surgery clearly had a positive effect as Do Your Job returned from a nine-week break to fare best of the rest behind the highly-promising My Drogo in the Premier Novices' Hurdle at Kelso in March, running at least as well as previously despite proving no match for the winner. He then signed off with the aforementioned runner-up effort in Liverpool, when splitting Belfast Banter and Dusart. Barring the fourth-last, when getting in close and a little bit scruffy, Do Your Job jumped really slickly on the good to soft ground at Aintree and battled bravely after the last to get within a length and a quarter of the Irish-trained winner, who was following up his County Hurdle triumph.

Ending the season on such a trajectory bodes extremely well for Do Your Job, especially having proved himself on far more testing ground in the autumn, and there is plenty about him to think he could be even better over fences in 2021/22. He won his only start in Irish points and his rangy physique also points to chasing being his true calling.

Michael Scudamore

Conclusion: *Likeable and progressive sort who reached a useful level over hurdles and should prove capable of better still in novice chases at up to 2½m*

Easy As That (Ire)   h130p
6 b.g. Sans Frontieres (Ire) – Bell Storm (Ire) (Glacial Storm (USA))
2020/21 h17v² h16d⁴ h19v* Feb 5

Venetia Williams sending out wide-margin, heavy-ground handicap hurdle winners at Chepstow in February is nothing new, but there was something rather out of the ordinary about the performance of Easy As That who overcame a clumsy round of jumping.

Making his handicap debut over 19f at Chepstow after showing promise over 2m on his first two starts over hurdles, Easy As That was evidently thought capable of defying an opening BHA mark of 114 (sent off the 85/40 favourite) and duly didn't disappoint. He made several mistakes on his way round but was simply too well treated for the others, proving suited by the longer trip and tapping into the ability which saw him impress in winning bumpers at Ffos Las and Musselburgh in 2019/20. He was eased down close home and still passed the post with nine lengths to spare over the doughty runner-up Eamon An Cnoic, with a yawning 24 lengths back to the third Electron Bleu.

Easy As That will need to improve his jumping if he's to fulfil all his considerable potential, but that will hopefully come as he gains in experience, while stepping up to 3m is also entitled to bring about further progress. Easy As That's dam, Bell Storm, was a winning pointer, while she is a half-sister to Time For Rupert, who was runner-up to Big Buck's in the 2010 Stayers' Hurdle prior to winning three times as a chaser.

A revised BHA mark of 130—fully 16 lb higher than when successful at Chepstow—doesn't look insurmountable should Easy As That's connections decide to continue over hurdles, but his long-term future almost certainly lies over fences. Still only a six-year-old, he has plenty of time on his side and, whichever discipline he tackles in 2021/22, there are plenty of nice prizes to be aimed at during the depths of winter given how effective he is in the mud. *Venetia Williams*

Conclusion: *Slow learner who looked well above-average when routing the opposition on his handicap debut over hurdles; has the physique (plenty of scope) to take well to chasing and could make hay in soft-ground novice chases at up to 3m*

 ## Eaton Collina (Ire)   h111

6 b.g. Milan – Flowers On Sunday (Ire) (Presenting)
2020/21 h16d² h20s³ h16g :: 2021/22 h20d³ May 10

Kerry Lee—together with her father, Richard, before the training licence was passed on—needs very little introduction when it comes to the matter of improving horses as they move into handicap chases. In an effort to help hammer the point home, however, see the following list which details the discrepancy in pounds between each particular stable representative's opening BHA mark over hurdles and their peak rating as chasers: Happy Diva–39 lb, Mountainous–36 lb, Russe Blanc–35 lb, Top Gamble–27 lb, Bishops Road–26 lb, Kylemore Lough–21 lb and Storm Control–15 lb.

It is obviously far too soon to suggest that the lightly raced Eaton Collina could be on a similar trajectory to some of those past and present stable stars. In fact, his opening BHA mark of 114 over hurdles has been reduced slightly to 109 following his two runs in handicap company to date, firstly when beating only a couple of rivals home in a 13-runner novice handicap at Newbury in March and then when third—this time beaten 11 lengths—in an open handicap at Ffos Las in May.

Eaton Collina had previously shown definite signs of promise, though, including when third behind the fairly useful Optimise Prime on his final qualifying run in a novice hurdle at Hereford in December. Sent off the 2/1 favourite on that occasion, with the move up to 2½m on soft ground expected to play to his strengths, Eaton Collina showed fair form to be beaten less than seven lengths despite the run of the race working against him (unsuited by the emphasis on speed in a steadily-run affair).

Eaton Collina should have more offer as he gains in experience and moving up in distance again looks a given at some stage judged on his profile so far. However, it is not until tackling handicaps over fences that we'll really know how good he could be, hopefully taking off like so many horses from his stable before him. He'll be eligible for low-grade novice handicap chases in the autumn and should have little trouble winning one of those before progressing through the ranks. *Kerry Lee*

Conclusion: *Showed only fair form over hurdles but gained valuable experience ahead of a quick switch to fences; likely to prove a different proposition in novice handicap chases over 2½m+*

Simon Walker (Eaton Collina): *"A 16% strike rate with chasers compared to 10% with hurdlers over the last five seasons is indicative of the way the Kerry Lee yard focuses on chasing types, Eaton Collina a smashing example of the sort of horse that will do appreciably better when faced with larger obstacles. He qualified for a mark after a couple of placed efforts in novices and, though third was the best he managed in a couple of handicaps in the spring, it'll be most surprising if he doesn't leave that form behind when his attention is turned to chasing."*

Elle Est Belle   b106
5 b.m. Fame And Glory – Katalina (Hernando (Fr))
2020/21 F17d* F16v* F16d³ F17d² Apr 8

The Dawn Run Mares' Novices' Hurdle has been run at the Cheltenham Festival since 2016 and all six winners up to this point have been trained in Ireland. Willie Mullins won each of the first five renewals courtesy of Limini (2016), Let's Dance (2017), Laurina (2018), Eglantine du Seuil (2019) and Concertista (2020), while the 2021 heroine, Telmesomethinggirl, was saddled by Henry de Bromhead, who ended up having an extraordinary week at Prestbury Park in March.

If one were to draw up a list of upwardly-mobile British trainers most likely to muscle in on the action when it comes to this race in particular, granted the right ammunition, then Dan Skelton would probably sit top. And, in the shape of Elle Est Belle, the Skelton operation have the raw materials to ultimately mount a bold bid on that so far elusive spring target.

Elle Est Belle made four appearances in her first season and emerged with a Timeform bumper rating of 106 having won her first two (including a dead-heat in a listed mares' event at Cheltenham's November meeting) before hitting the frame in graded company at both the Cheltenham and Aintree Festivals in the spring. Her third in the Champion Bumper was a superb effort given where she raced in comparison to the pair who beat her, Sir Gerhard and Kilcruit, while in hindsight Harry Skelton may have waited just a fraction too long to launch his challenge when Elle Est Belle couldn't quite reel in Me Too Please in the Grade 2 mares' bumper on the opening day of the Grand National meeting.

That was still another highly creditable performance and one which certainly left the neutral observer wanting more. That will come in the novice hurdling ranks and, while clearly capable of holding her own against male counterparts, it would be understandable were connections looking to plot a route sticking to her own sex ahead of a Dawn Run showdown with the Irish battalions. **Dan Skelton**

Conclusion: *Useful bumper mare who could rack up a sequence in novice hurdles against her own sex in Britain before tackling the best of the Irish in the Dawn Run at Cheltenham*

Farinet (Fr) c139p

6 gr.g. Lord Du Sud (Fr) – Mendy Tennise (Fr) (Kadalko (Fr))
2020/21 c19s³ c19d² c20v³ c20s* Mar 13

Farinet has already changed hands a couple of times, but it is hoped he now gets a clear shot at his racing having produced a career-best performance when winning a handicap chase over 2½m on his final outing at Sandown in March. Initially trained by Guy Cherel before gaining most of his experience over hurdles and fences in his native France for Yannick Fouin, Farinet cost his current connections €52,000 at the Arqana Deauville Summer Sale in July 2020 and early evidence suggests it could turn out to be money well spent.

Farinet raced only twice for the Venetia Williams yard during the latest season, building on a promising Haydock third in February to win going away in the driving Esher rain three weeks later, a victory which saw his BHA mark rise 9 lb from 125 to 134. Admittedly, the bare form of the Sandown race can be questioned to some extent—the runner-up Up The Straight and third Lust For Glory didn't do much to enhance it with subsequent no-shows at Cheltenham and Aintree respectively—but it had looked a deep enough race on paper beforehand, with six of the nine runners who went to post having won on their previous start. In the end, it turned into a gruelling examination of stamina and all bar the front two had effectively cried enough a fair way from the finish, Farinet being headed between the final two fences before responding generously for Charlie Deutsch under his light weight after the last to score by six and a half lengths.

Soft ground looks something of a pre-requisite for Farinet, who was raced solely on soft or worse during his nine-race spell across the Channel. Williams excels with such horses and will continue to do so no doubt, so look out for Farinet when the going gets tough in the dark winter months. His proven ability to cope so well with the Railway fences at Sandown will not be lost on his shrewd trainer, who often targets staying handicaps at the course, and there should still be a little mileage in this horse's revised mark when conditions are suitable. ***Venetia Williams***

Conclusion: *French import with just two runs under his belt for new connections; must have soft ground and likely to improve again when stepped up to 3m*

Flagrant Delitiep (Fr)   c135p

6 gr.g. Fragrant Mix (Ire) – Naltiepy (Fr) (Dom Alco (Fr))
2020/21 c20g⁴ c20d² c20s* c21s* c20v² Feb 20

If you had to sculpt a National Hunt horse who was merely biding his time as a hurdler before being sent chasing, it is reasonable to suggest Flagrant Delitiep could be the end result. The sizeable son of Fragrant Mix is a brother to five-time winner Altiepix and a half-brother to Eurotiep, who has started to make something of an impression for Ireland's champion trainer Willie Mullins, though in terms of family traits perhaps he has more resemblance to his dam's half-sister Pomme Tiepy, also trained by Mullins, who won five of her first six starts over fences between June 2007 and February 2008.

Flagrant Delitiep wasn't quite so prolific during the latest season, but he did his level best with two wins and two near-misses from his handful of public appearances. He began the campaign on a BHA mark of 113 but was immediately dropped 3 lb following a laboured comeback run at Wincanton in October, with the emphasis on speed on good ground offering a plausible excuse. Flagrant Delitiep duly left that form behind when faced with softer going on his next two starts over the same course and distance, finishing a staying-on second (beaten just a length) behind the experienced Native Robin in November before comprehensively reversing that form on 2 lb better terms the following month.

Flagrant Delitiep defied a 9 lb higher mark to double his tally at Hereford four weeks later and, having been bumped up another 10 lb to a BHA mark of 131, he signed off with another career-best effort in defeat when beaten just half a length back at Wincanton in February. Having to miss the third last can't have helped him given his bold-jumping style, while he still arguably shaped like the best horse at the weights, idling slightly when hitting the front on the run-in and not having enough time to respond after being collared by the rallying Aintree My Dream close home.

Now rated 135, Flagrant Delitiep will be forced into slightly better company in 2021/22 and will need to keep on improving like he did during the latest season, but he's still only six and could conceivably be just coming into his own. ***Robert Walford***

Conclusion: *Progressive sort who shaped best when narrowly beaten at Wincanton on his final outing of last season; remains on a good mark with further improvement not out of the question when stepping up to 3m*

Matt Brocklebank (Flagrant Delitiep): *"One could be forgiven for lazily expecting the handicapper to have caught up with Robert Walford's Flagrant Delitiep, having moved him up from 110 to 135 by the time his season came to an end in February 2021, but I expect that assumption to prove some way wide of the mark. When winning at Wincanton and Hereford, the giant Flagrant Delitiep did so with plenty to spare, while he still arguably shaped like the best horse in the race when second—beaten half a length having idled on the run-in—when last sighted. There's a chance he'll stay 3m but the six-year-old has plenty more to offer in 2½m handicap chases when the mud is flying."*

Flash Collonges (Fr) h141p

6 b.g. Saddler Maker (Ire) – Prouesse Collonges (Fr) (Apple Tree (Fr))
2020/21 h22d* h21g^F h21s² h21s* h21d* Mar 6

The heavy fall suffered by Flash Collonges on just his second outing over hurdles could easily have dented such a young horse's confidence, so to see him build back up so quickly to win two of his three subsequent starts augurs very well for the future.

That crunching fourth-flight tumble came less than a month after his debut success in a novice hurdle at Exeter in November, where he won by three quarters of a length and seemingly surprised his connections in doing so (returned an SP of 10/1 after proving easy to back). In a steadily-run affair on ground described by Timeform as good to soft, Flash Collonges raced powerfully in mid-division before the race began in earnest on the home turn, a relative test of speed looking far from ideal. To his credit, however, Flash Collonges responded to every call from Harry Cobden and soon found himself in front on the approach to the last. A surprise success, but no fluke about it.

Flash Collonges showed no ill effects from his Doncaster fall with an improved display when beaten just half a length into second at Newbury in December, being picked off by the patiently-ridden French Paradoxe (disappointing since), and a similar performance was good enough to see him resume winning ways over 21f at Wincanton the following month. A subsequent break of 56 days followed but the result was the same and there was far more substance to the form of his handicap victory at Kelso in early-March, powering away from the final flight before idling close home, ultimately winning by six and a half lengths from a next-time-out winner.

There must be a very real chance the short time away from the track helped Flash Collonges grow into his considerable frame, in which case it's hard to imagine quite what he could become with another summer on his back. He is a very typical Paul Nicholls project in many ways, clearly learning on the job but getting the results along the way, too. From the same family as Grand National winner Neptune Collonges, Flash Collonges is likely to stay 3m and it's encouraging that he reached the standard he did over hurdles given that he's expected to come into his own over fences. *Paul Nicholls*

Conclusion: *Won three of his four completed starts in novice hurdles and appeals as very much one to keep on the right side when his attentions are switched to fences*

Flic Ou Voyou (Fr) h135

7 b.g. Kapgarde (Fr) – Hillflower (Fr) (Sabrehill (USA))
2020/21 h16g* h17d* h15g* h16s³ h16d² F18s⁵ h16d³ h16g² Apr 24

As a second-season novice, Flic Ou Voyou wasted no time in putting his experience to good use during the early stages of the latest campaign, winning his first three races, including a 23-length demolition job when reappearing at Chepstow's valuable early-

Flic Ou Voyou thrived on a busy campaign in 2020/21

October meeting. He doubled up at Newton Abbot just two days later before returning to Wincanton—where he'd recorded his two bumper victories as a four-year-old—to complete the hat-trick when long odds-on this time at 25/1-on.

On all three occasions Flic Ou Voyou was competing in fields of nine or fewer runners and on all three occasions he successfully made the running, so despite failing to add to his tally in five more outings during the 2020/21 campaign, two things really stand out ahead of an imminent switch to novice chasing. Firstly, he will be perfectly suited by small-field events in which he can dominate tactically and, secondly, he will probably be one earmarked by Paul Nicholls as likely to make hay before the ground turns during the depths of winter.

It's not that Flic Ou Voyou doesn't handle cut—he was beaten just a head on heavy at Taunton in December 2019— but his best performances have all been achieved on decent going and Timeform rated his second behind Herbiers under a big weight (was conceding 18 lb to the winner) on good ground in the Novices' Championship Final at Sandown in April as a career-best effort.

That's a great sign that the seven-year-old son of Kapgarde—the same sire Nicholls has already had success with in the chasing ranks courtesy of Clan des Obeaux, Dolos and As de Mee— is yet to fully reach his peak and there should be plenty of opportunities for him over fences. ***Paul Nicholls***

Conclusion: *Gained plenty of experience over hurdles and should be ready to roll early in the season before the bad ground arrives; likely to be seen to good effect in small-field novice chases*

Frero Banbou (Fr)   c137

6 b.g. Apsis – Lady Banbou (Fr) (Useful (Fr))
2020/21 h16d c18v³ c16v³ c16d* c16d⁴ Apr 8

Venetia Williams' success with French imports went up a few gears following the victory of Mon Mome at 100/1 in the 2009 Grand National. Since then she has trained horses of the calibre of Houblon des Obeaux, Rigadin de Beauchene, Katenko, Aso, Yala Enki, Cepage and, most recently, Royale Pagaille, all of whom were successful in graded company for the Kings Caple yard.

Frero Banbou could well be one of the next cabs off the rank for Williams, the six-year-old having benefitted from a wind procedure and a near three-month break in March when he returned at Sandown with a decisive victory by nine lengths. Stepped up in class after that, he contested the Red Rum Handicap Chase at Aintree, racing on the speed and only giving way two from home. Left in fourth at the last following the heavy fall of Getaway Trump, Frero Banbou kept on well to secure that position and the form was somewhat franked when the second home, Sully D'Oc AA, went on to win at the Punchestown Festival.

Frero Banbou's main attributes include his very good jumping, which should stand him in good stead in 2m handicap chases as he makes his way up the ladder. He has also shown plenty of speed in his races, allowing him to travel smoothly, so he really does look like an out-and-out 2m chaser at this stage. A winner on very soft ground at Auteuil when trained by Gabriel Leenders, Frero Banbou's exploits on a better surface in Britain in the spring suggest versatility when it comes to ground conditions. A strong and sturdy-looking gelding, he's a half-brother to three winners including the Willie Mullins-trained Tango Banbou. ***Venetia Williams***

Conclusion: *Has the skillset, profile and potential to progress through the ranks in 2m handicap chases*

Gericault Roque (Fr)   h123

5 b.g. Montmartre (Fr) – Nijinska Delaroque (Fr) (Lute Antique (Fr))
2020/21 F17v² h16s* h20v³ h16s* Mar 12

Montmartre, a Group 1-winning son of Montjeu, has been an excellent source of National Hunt horses in recent years, including the likes of Labaik, Elimay, Capitaine and Bigmartre, the winners of over £500,000 in prize money between them.

Looking at Montmartre's youngsters coming through, Gericault Roque offered plenty to work on as he recorded two wins from four starts in his first season under Rules. Having graduated from an Irish point, he finished second on his debut for the David Pipe yard in a Newton Abbot bumper in October, showing fair form whilst shaping as if needing a stiffer test. He then spent 11 weeks on the sidelines (during which time he had a breathing operation) before his hurdling bow at Plumpton in January, where a tongue strap was added to the hood he had worn on his debut under Rules. In a good quality maiden run at an end-to-end gallop, the three market principals had it between them some way out, with Gericault Roque getting going late to beat the free-going favourite Natural History (another member of the *Fifty*) by half a length.

The same headgear combination was utilised in a novice hurdle at Fakenham five weeks later, but Gericault Roque could manage only third this time, passing the post around 14 lengths behind the useful Shang Tang at a track which looked sharp enough for him. Gericault Roque then made his handicap debut from a BHA mark of 117 at Sandown in March, going the other way around, over a shorter trip and with all the headgear removed. Timeform reported the ground to be soft and they went quick enough in the conditions, with Gericault Roque capitalising on a mistake two out from Starvoski as he stayed on up the hill to record a convincing nine-and-a-half length victory.

Gericault Roque's dam was a 17f chase winner in France and so was his half-brother, Balou de la Roque, so fences look like being this horse's eventual calling. However, he looks to have unfinished business over hurdles in the meantime and remains one to be positive about in handicaps. Both his wins came at 2m, but 2½m remains likely to suit him better. **David Pipe**

Conclusion: *Twice a winner during his first season over hurdles and highly unlikely to have finished improving just yet; looks the sort to win more handicaps from a BHA mark of 124*

Go Dante   b110

5 b.g. Kayf Tara – Whoops A Daisy (Definite Article)
2020/21 F15s* Mar 11

When Olly Murphy picked up Angel of Harlem from Mark Bradstock in the summer of 2018, she had raced five times without troubling the judge. The change in surroundings triggered immediate improvement, though, and she won on her stable debut for Murphy at Market Rasen, setting in motion a run of success which saw her record five wins and three seconds from 14 starts for the yard.

Therefore, it should have come as no surprise that Murphy was keen to get his hands on her half-brother, Go Dante, who made a big impression on his one and only start during the latest season, when he cantered to a smooth success in a bumper at Wincanton in March. The Grade 2 bumper at Aintree's Grand National Festival was considered after that but, in the end, Go Dante was roughed off for the season with his unbeaten record still firmly intact.

Owned by Mrs Barbara Hester of Brewin'Upastorm fame for the same yard, hopes will be high that Go Dante can emulate the career path of his stablemate. Brewin'Upastorm won convincingly on his novice hurdling debut before competing three times at the highest level in his freshman season, a campaign which culminated with him finishing fourth in the Ballymore Novices' Hurdle at the Cheltenham Festival and second in the Mersey Novices' Hurdle at Aintree.

Connections are likely to have similarly lofty aspirations for Go Dante, particularly as his Wincanton bumper win came in a race which has a recent history of producing good horses, with Lalor and One For The Team winning it in 2017 and 2018 respectively. Not only was his half-sister, Angel of Harlem, a prolific winner, but his dam was useful over hurdles as well, with a listed mares' event at Kempton featuring amongst her five wins for Nicky Henderson. *Olly Murphy*

Conclusion: *Must be considered an exciting prospect for novice hurdles judged on his pedigree and the excellent impression he created on his sole start in bumpers*

Green Book (Fr)   h117p

4 b.g. Authorized (Ire) – Mantissa (Oratorio (Ire))
2020/21 h16v² Feb 17

Green Book is only four, but he's had an eventful career already. Firstly, he raced five times for Brian Ellison as a two-year-old, running well several times without winning. Secondly, he then raced eight times for Patrick Monfort on the Flat in France, finishing second three times but still failing to get his head in front. And, most recently, he joined the Venetia Williams yard in early-2021, finishing second on his one and only hurdling start over 2m at Hereford in February.

That's as far as his career in the world of National Hunt racing has got, but there have been some clues on the Flat this summer that Williams has got herself a useful recruit for staying novice hurdles in 2021/22. His all-the-way win at Chester's May Festival stands out, especially as it remains his one and only career success so far. Rated 77 and racing off a light weight under Roodee specialist Franny Norton, Green Book received glowing praise from his veteran jockey who beamed "he couldn't have done it any better" following a comfortable success by nearly five lengths. No more Flat wins have followed in three runs, but good performances off marks in the high 80s at Ascot and Goodwood bode well ahead of an inevitable winter campaign.

The last two runs of his career on the Flat have come over 2½m+, so staying novice hurdles look like being his game in the coming months. Outpaced over 2m at Hereford in February, subsequent events suggest he did well to run second over the minimum trip that day. Green Book is out of a mare who gained listed success on the Flat in Italy and by Authorised, whose success in the jumping world is magnified by the exploits of his flagbearer son, Tiger Roll. **Venetia Williams**

Conclusion: *A successful Flat campaign coupled with a promising Hereford hurdling debut over an inadequate trip hints at a fruitful season in staying novice hurdles*

Guard Your Dreams   h143

5 b.g. Fame And Glory – Native Sunrise (Ire) (Definite Article)
2020/21 h17s* h17v⁴ h17v* h16s* h16d⁶ h21d h20d³ Apr 10

Winning handicaps with horses who had already run in graded novice events is very Nigel Twiston-Davies. Think Ballyandy, Splash of Ginge, Flying Angel, Ballybolley, Blaklion and Cogry, to name just a few. Cogry, a nine-time winner for the yard before his retirement last October, carried the familiar red, black and yellow silks of Graham and Alison Jelley, the owners who have another promising handicapper to go to war with in 2021/22 in the shape of Guard Your Dreams.

Having had just the eight runs in his career, one bumper and seven hurdles races, Guard Your Dream remains suitably unexposed and he improved throughout his novice hurdling campaign, culminating with a career-best effort when third behind My Drogo on his final start in the Mersey Novices' Hurdle at Aintree. That performance suggested he's perhaps not a top-level performer in the making but very much a handicapper with a bright future.

After learning his trade at the left-handed and sharp Bangor-On-Dee, Guard Your Dreams first showed signs of real promise when winning at that course in a first-time hood in November, just about making all for a clear-cut success by 10 lengths. Plunged into handicap company after that, he defied a BHA mark of 128 on his debut in that sphere at Sandown in January before being put away for the best part of two months ahead of tougher assignments. Sixth in the Betfair Hurdle at Newbury, a race Twiston-Davies has a fabulous record in thanks to the likes of Splash of Ginge and Ballyandy, he then shaped better than the bare result when seventh in the Coral Cup at the Cheltenham Festival, getting caught further back than ideal and having to fight his way through traffic after a slow start.

Rated 140 ahead of the new campaign following his third at Aintree, the good-topped Guard Your Dreams will be worth keeping on the right side in handicap hurdles at around 2½m in 2021/22. Related to Carys' Commodity and The Jigsaw Man, two winners who excelled over the intermediate trip, he looks tough, genuine and well-equipped for the tasks ahead. **Nigel Twiston-Davies**

Conclusion: *Still looks ahead of his mark and should be competitive in the more valuable handicap hurdles at around 2½m in his second season over timber*

Hillcrest (Ire) b100

6 br.g. Stowaway – Shop Dj (Ire) (Dushyantor (USA))
2020/21 F17s² F16d* Mar 23

Henry Daly wouldn't be renowned for having bumper winners. Indeed, in 2019 and 2020, the yard had just one winner from 29 runners in such races and the man himself probably reacted with a mere shrug of the shoulders. It's not his thing. So, when he gets one that's good enough to win a bumper, it's probably worth sitting up and taking notice, particularly when they have the imposing physique of Hillcrest.

By Stowaway, a stallion responsible for Cheltenham Festival winners like Monkfish and Put The Kettle On, Hillcrest looks every inch a future chaser, but he's in the *Fifty* in anticipation of making the grade in staying novice hurdles. This is more Daly's thing and it's not long ago that he navigated a successful campaign in similar company with Stoney Mountain, also owned by Trevor Hemmings, who won twice, was twice placed in Grade 2 events and ran at the Cheltenham Festival in 2018/19.

A similar sort of schedule could well lie in wait for Hillcrest after two promising runs in bumpers. He was beaten just a nose when second on his debut at Doncaster in November, looking raw but still pushing a well-touted fellow debutant all the way, and that form had been well advertised by the time he made his next start at Wetherby in March. He was sent off the 5/4 favourite on the last occasion and ultimately did enough to get off the mark, though that doesn't tell the whole story as he hit a high of 920 in-running before sprouting wings to collar Armand de Brignac in the final strides. He was clearly far from the finished article, but it's encouraging that he was still able to win and his strength at the finish suggests he'll be suited by 2½m+ in novice hurdles.

Hillcrest is out of Shop Dj, who won a point and a bumper before winning twice, including in Grade 3 company, during her first season over hurdles. She would go on to win over fences as well for Peter Fahey, but she was arguably better over timber. Hillcrest is also a half-brother to Bold Record, trained by Nicky Henderson, who won on his second start over hurdles over 2½m at Uttoxeter. ***Henry Daly***

Conclusion: *Caught the eye in bumpers for a yard not renowned for success in that sphere, identifying him as a staying novice hurdler to follow in 2021/22*

Hitman (Fr) c152p

5 b.g. Falco (USA) – Tercah Girl (Fr) (Martaline)
2020/21 c16v* c16d² c20vᶠ c20g* c20d³ Apr 8

Sir Alex Ferguson and Ged Mason had some day at Aintree on April 8, 2021. The high-profile owners were involved with the first three winners on the card—all in Grade 1 races—as Protektorat, Monmiral and Clan des Obeaux swept all before them. For good measure, they were also represented by the third-placed horse in the Manifesto Novices'

Chase won by Protektorat, with Hitman arguably shaping like the best horse in the race before his stamina ran out late on.

A French import from Guillaume Macaire, Hitman was sent straight over fences as a four-year-old by Paul Nicholls and duly bolted up by 30 lengths on his British debut at Ffos Las in November. That performance earned him a step up in grade for the Henry VIII Novices' Chase at Sandown the following month, a mighty assignment on just his second start for the yard. He ran a huge race under the circumstances but couldn't overhaul Allmankind, another four-year-old who had the benefit of plenty of experience over hurdles the previous season. Beaten only two and a half lengths, Hitman certainly did his reputation no harm and offered plenty to work on for the rest of the campaign.

Hitman reappeared two months later in the Scilly Isles Novices' Chase at the same course, another Grade 1 in which he was going well when falling at the twelfth. The Cheltenham Festival was unlikely to be on the agenda anyway, but that mishap reinforced Nicholls' view that Hitman wasn't ready for that test as such an early stage in his development, preferring to get a confidence-boosting success at Newbury under his belt before heading to Aintree. Back in a much more competitive race in the Manifesto, he travelled strongly for a long way before getting tired, passing the post four lengths behind the winner whilst leaving the impression there is more to come from him when dropping back down slightly in trip.

A tall gelding who has had wind surgery, Hitman is the first foal out of a French 2m winner over hurdles. He already looks the best progeny of dual-purpose sire Falco and there will almost certainly be more good races to be won with him in 2021/22. He should stay 2½m on an easy track but is likely to prove best at shorter, with a race such as the Haldon Gold Cup at Exeter appealing as a suitable starting point. **Paul Nicholls**

Conclusion: *Showed smart form as a novice chaser and still young enough to suggest he can go on improving; sure to win more good races for a yard with few peers when it comes to spotting winnable opportunities*

Killer Clown (Ire)   c141

7 b.g. Getaway (Ger) – Our Soiree (Ire) (Milan)
2020/21 c22d^{ur} c24d^6 c20d^3 c20d* c20g^2 c20g^3 Apr 24

Point winner Killer Clown's background and physique suggested that he would come into his own when going chasing and he proved as much in the latest season, quickly developing into a useful handicapper. He showed significant run-by-run improvement in the early part of the campaign and was an impressive winner of a 2½m novice handicap chase at Kempton on Boxing Day, beating a promising rival, Falco Blitz, by seven and a half lengths with the pair 16 lengths clear of the remainder.

Killer Clown was hit with a 15 lb rise in the weights and faced a much stiffer task on his next outing in the prestigious Greatwood Gold Cup at Newbury, but he raised his game again to grab second, finding only another unexposed novice, Umbrigado, too strong on the run-in. Given the sharp upward curve Killer Clown had been tracking, his final effort of the season, when beaten more than 12 lengths in third at Sandown, would have been disappointing if taken at face value. However, it's easy to make excuses as the race developed into a sprint from the third-last and he was shuffled back on the home turn as the tempo was lifting. He is better than he was able to show at Sandown and looks up to making an impact in the major 2½m handicap chases. *Emma Lavelle*

Conclusion: *Progressive chaser who could have more to offer in his second season over fences and is one to note in valuable 2½m handicaps like the Paddy Power Gold Cup*

Lesser (Ire)   h131p
7 b.g. Stowaway – Aine Dubh (Ire) (Bob Back (USA))
2020/21 F17v* h20d* :: 2021/22 h21g* May 5

Richard Phillips has an exciting prospect on his hands in the shape of Lesser, who is unbeaten in four starts (three under Rules) and still has scope for plenty of improvement. A winner of his sole start in Irish points, he made his first appearance for Phillips in a Bangor bumper in December, a race which was run on heavy winter ground and inevitably turned into a gruelling contest for inexperienced youngsters. Lesser's point experience counted for a lot under the circumstances and he showed deep reserves of stamina to power clear in the final furlong and win by 11 lengths.

Subsequent events showed that Lesser is far from just a mudlark, though. He was given a three-month break before his hurdling debut at Wetherby and, stepped up to 2½m on good to soft ground, he produced a very taking display to maintain his unbeaten record. Hurdling fluently and travelling strongly, he came through to lead two out and already had the prize in safekeeping when nearest challenger Ballycallan Flame departed at the last.

Lesser's final outing came on good ground at Kelso in May and resulted in another fluent win despite him having to concede weight to all bar one of his rivals. Admittedly, it probably wasn't the deepest contest, but Lesser was taken on for the lead this time and it was hard not to be taken by the way he then drew clear in the straight, just needing to be kept up to his work as he produced his best effort yet to win by 15 lengths.

A strong and lengthy gelding, Lesser is going to flourish when going beyond 2½m over fences. An opening BHA mark of 130 appeals as being very attractive and he's one his excellent team look set to have plenty of fun with in the coming months. *Richard Phillips*

Conclusion: *Successful in all three starts under Rules by a cumulative margin of 51 lengths; already useful and rates a cracking prospect for novice chasing*

Luttrell Lad (Ire)   b106

5 b.g. Beat Hollow – Fairly Definite (Ire) (Definite Article)
2020/21 F16m² F17g* F16s* F17d⁴ :: 2021/22 h16g* Sep 13

It's a season of change at Sandhill Stables following the retirement of Richard Johnson. The former champion jockey hung up his saddle in April after a remarkable career which saw him ride 3,819 winners. For over two decades he was associated with the Philip Hobbs stable, partnering Rooster Booster and Flagship Uberalles to memorable Cheltenham Festival victories along the way. Big winners have been a little in short supply in recent seasons for the yard, but long-term second rider Tom O'Brien has still inherited a lucrative role and, in the shape of Luttrell Lad, he has a horse who could go a long way over timber.

Luttrell Lad didn't get everything right in four starts in bumpers in 2020/21, but he showed a useful level of ability, with the promise of more to come as he steps up in trip over hurdles. He looked unlucky not to finish closer and possibly even win when second (beaten two lengths) on his debut at Stratford last September, only getting a gap when it was too late. He was unable to peg back the winner but managed to put eight lengths between himself and the third inside the final furlong, doing so without coming under maximum pressure. It was an effort full of promise and Luttrell Lad showed the benefit of that experience when getting off the mark on his next outing at Market Rasen in November, still looking far from the finished article (raced keenly) but sticking to his task well to land the spoils by two and three quarter lengths.

Luttrell Lad was more impressive when defying a penalty at Taunton in March, with keenness again failing to impact on his finishing effort as he quickened clear to win by three and a quarter lengths. That performance earned him a step up in class for the Grade 2 bumper at Aintree's Grand National Festival, a race run on less testing ground in which Luttrell Lad seemed to find things happening a shade too quickly. He settled a bit better than he had previously in a first-time hood, though, and the way he stayed on to finish a clear fourth reinforced the view that he will be suited by 2½m over timber. Already off the mark over hurdles at Worcester in September, there are plenty of races to be won with him. **Phillip Hobbs**

Conclusion: *Often raced keenly in bumpers and must have a big engine to still emerge with two wins from four starts; looks sure to progress and win novice hurdles over 2½m+*

Martello Sky   h125

5 gr.m. Martaline – Kentucky Sky (Cloudings (Ire))
2020/21 F16d* F16v⁵ h16d* h17s* h17d h20g* Apr 15

Martello Sky racked up four wins from six starts during the latest season, with her two defeats coming when her sights were raised for a listed mares' bumper and the Dawn Run Mares' Novices' Hurdle, both at Cheltenham. Her hurdling let her down on the last

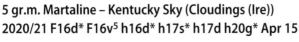

occasion, causing her to lose her pitch before the third last, but she stayed on well from the home turn to finish eighth (beaten around 14 lengths) behind Telmesomethinggirl.

Martello Sky headed to the Festival unbeaten over hurdles following successive wins at Fakenham in December and Market Rasen in February. She showed a good change of gear at Fakenham to beat Allavina, who had finished one place in front of her in the Cheltenham bumper the time before, by three and a quarter lengths despite jumping sketchily. Martello Sky was better in that department at Market Rasen where she travelled strongly through the race and, having made her challenge at the second last, she asserted in the final 100 yards to win comfortably by a length and a quarter.

It's no wonder connections were tempted into a tilt at the Dawn Run and, while that didn't quite work out, Martello Sky did end the season with another victory at Cheltenham in April, the most significant win of her career to date in a listed novice hurdle against her own sex. Stepping up to 2½m for the first time, she again travelled well and just needed to be driven out on the run-in to beat Sandymount Rose by two and three quarter lengths.

That wasn't a strong test at the trip and Martello Sky is far from short of speed, but it's encouraging that she has shown her versatility with regards distance, opening up more options in 2021/22. She is already a prolific winner and has the physique to make at least as good a chaser if connections opt to make a quick switch, too. ***Lucy Wadham***

Conclusion: *Likeable mare who boasts a good strike rate with five wins from eight starts in bumpers/over hurdles; has the scope to take well to chasing and will remain of interest whatever the chosen route*

My Drogo h156p

6 b.g. Milan – My Petra (Midnight Legend)
2020/21 F16s² h16g* h16s* h18d* h20d* Apr 10

Such was the Irish dominance of the Cheltenham novice hurdles, My Drogo's Grade 1 success at Aintree came as a huge fillip to the beleaguered British ranks, producing a very smart performance in the manner of one who could scale even greater heights over fences in 2021/22.

Dan Skelton's rise to become a serious contender for the trainers' title has been one of the stories of recent seasons and here he has a horse anyone would dream of having in the yard. Even as early as December Skelton was struggling to hide his enthusiasm for the rising star, saying after his winning hurdling debut at Newbury: "He's as high as anything we've had on raw ability but chasing will be his game. He's very talented and could be up there with anyone's best this season."

It's fair to say that My Drogo lived up to the hype as he ended the latest campaign as Timeform's highest-rated novice hurdler in Britain, some achievement given that his career only began in October, when he belied an SP of 50/1 to chase home I Am Maximus in a Cheltenham bumper. Hurdling quickly beckoned and the Newbury win was a taking

My Drogo swept all before him as a novice hurdler

one, travelling on the bridle for much of the contest before being produced to overhaul Saggazza in the closing stages. He looked sure to go on to better things and duly found a chunk of improvement a few weeks later at Ascot, defying a drift in the market to land the Kennel Gate Novices' Hurdle. My Drogo faced a battle-hardened rival in Llandinabo Lad and had to dig deep, but he was ultimately well on top at the finish, overcoming a mistake at the last to win comfortably by two and three quarter lengths.

The Cheltenham Festival was never on the agenda for My Drogo and instead he took his unbeaten record over timber to Kelso for the Premier Novices' Hurdle, a Grade 2 in which he gave his rivals weight and a sound beating, quickening clear from the second last to land the spoils by nine and a half lengths. That winning margin was to be repeated when he stepped up to the top level in the Mersey Novices' Hurdle at Aintree, travelling strongly throughout and powering clear late on to beat the useful Minella Drama with plenty in hand.

For My Drogo to achieve all this in his first season of racing was some achievement, but chasing was always going to be his game and a novice campaign is reportedly on the cards in 2021/22. He'll surely be amongst the best in the division given a clear run at things, especially as he has the speed to be effective in good company at 2m but with the promise of better to come upped in trip later in the campaign. **Dan Skelton**

Conclusion: *Improved with every start in novice hurdles and ended the campaign as the best in the division in Britain; a proper chasing type on looks and likely to develop into a leading contender for a race such as the Marsh Novices' Chase at the Cheltenham Festival*

Natural History   h128

6 b.g. Nathaniel (Ire) – Film Script (Unfuwain (USA))
2020/21 h16s² h15v² h16g* h16v⁶ h17g² Apr 13

Turned over at odds of 7/2-on on his final outing of the 2020/21 campaign, we don't make a habit of including horses such as Natural History in the *Fifty*, but the feeling remains that he still has unfinished business as a hurdler and could prove a worthy exception to that rule.

A progressive stayer on the Flat for Andrew Balding and The Queen, Natural History joined Gary Moore fresh from chasing home Euchen Glen in the St Simon Stakes at Newbury last October. He was sent off the 6/4-on favourite for his hurdling debut in a maiden at Plumpton in January but, having raced freely and been untidy at the fourth and second last, he was unable to repel the late thrust of fellow *Fifty* member Gericault Roque.

Natural History made his next start in a novice hurdle at Wincanton in February, a race which was dominated by Lucky One, who gave the free-going Natural History a jumping lesson along the way. The pair were separated by 20 lengths at the line and it had to go down as another disappointing effort from Natural History, though it did serve the purpose of getting him qualified for handicaps. Making his debut in that sphere at Plumpton the following month, he duly proved an opening BHA mark of 116 to be wholly inadequate as he made most of the running to win easily by 15 lengths, affording jockey Jamie Moore the luxury of easing him down close home.

The handicapper was swift to act and Natural History floundered following a 16 lb hike in the weights when down the field in the Imperial Cup at Sandown 12 days later. The deep ground on that occasion provided him with a plausible excuse, though, especially as he did too much too soon at the head of affairs before weakening from two out. Back in novice company at Newton Abbot in April, Natural History signed off with the aforementioned defeat at long odds-on, a race he probably would have won but for a costly mistake (not his first of the race) at the final flight.

Nevertheless, Natural History will begin the 2021/22 campaign on a BHA mark of 126, 6 lb lower than when running at Sandown. That leaves him with a bit of room for manoeuvre and there is every chance he will kick on during his second season over hurdles, with the level he achieved on the Flat giving cause for plenty of optimism in that regard. A free-going sort, he handled very testing ground on the level but probably isn't a strong enough stayer to handle it in this sphere, with 2m handicap hurdles away from bad going likely to prove his optimum conditions. *Gary Moore*

Conclusion: Needs to learn to settle but showed borderline smart form on the Flat and could yet reach a similar level over hurdles granted a sound surface in 2m handicaps

Oscar Elite (Ire)   h136

6 b.g. Oscar (Ire) – Lady Elite (Ire) (Lord Americo)

2020/21 h19s* h24s* h21v h17v³ h24d² h25d³ Apr 9

With several high-profile horses performing below their best, the 2020/21 campaign was a testing one for Colin Tizzard and particularly frustrating given that it was his last full season training in his own name. That will be but a footnote when reflecting on Tizzard's training career in years to come, though, and when he does hand the licence over to son Joe, he'll do so having trained 32 Grade 1 winners and some great names along the way.

It's a tough act for his long-time assistant to follow, but there are some promising young horses ready to step forward under his tutelage, perhaps none more so than Oscar Elite. He ran six times in his first season over hurdles, winning novice events at Chepstow on his first two outings before taking another step forward to fill the runner-up spot behind Vanillier in the Albert Bartlett Novices' Hurdle at the Cheltenham Festival.

For Oscar Elite to do that in a campaign when his trainer's string was struggling to build momentum looks significant, and there was certainly lots to like about his Festival run. Wearing a first-time tongue strap on his first try at 3m, he was one of the last off the bridle and, after making headway two out, stayed on steadily to pass the post 11 lengths adrift of the enterprisingly-ridden winner. Oscar Elite then hit the frame again at Grade 1 level at Aintree's Grand National Festival, lacking the gears to trouble Ahoy Senor and Bravesmansgame in the Sefton Novices' Hurdle but still matching his Cheltenham run with another strong-staying effort in third.

Another from the Sub Lieutenant and Lord Windermere family, along with fellow *Fifty* member Demachine, everything about Oscar Elite screams chaser. He has the physique to thrive over the larger obstacles and, if taking to them as well as expected, must be regarded a very exciting prospect for all the good staying novices. Joe Tizzard will be looking for a big first season and here's a horse with whom he can already harbour Cheltenham and Aintree aspirations. ***Joe Tizzard***

Conclusion: Achieved a useful level of form in six starts over hurdles and has the pedigree/physique to suggest he can develop into a leading staying novice chaser in 2021/22

EVERY HORSE, EVERY RACE, EVERY DAY
Bet smarter with the ultimate form guide

Paso Doble (Ire)   h124p

4 br.g. Dawn Approach (Ire) – Baila Me (Ger) (Samum (Ger))
2020/21 h16g³ :: 2021/22 h16g* May 3

Strictly fans will know all about the paso doble—the fast-paced modern ballroom dance is popular with viewers and judges alike, or so Tess Daly tells us. The horse who carries the same name isn't short of speed, either, but he's included in this list in the expectation he will come into his own when stepped up to 2½m in the coming months.

Paso Doble has been in safe hands throughout his racing career, starting out with Jim Bolger on the Flat. He proved a tough and progressive handicapper, winning at Roscommon and Fairyhouse before being snapped up by his current connections for 125,000 guineas. Clearly that's not cheap, but he has shown plenty of promise in two starts over timber to date and the fact he was pitched in at the deep end for his hurdling debut, in the Adonis Juvenile Hurdle at Kempton in February, suggests he is held in high regard. He ran a hugely encouraging race at Kempton, too, recovering from a mistake at the third before making good late headway to hit the frame behind Tritonic.

Connections were already thinking long-term with Paso Doble after that run and he wasn't sighted again until getting off the mark in a novice hurdle back at Kempton in May. Bar a mistake at the second he hurdled well and, while not having to match the form he showed in the Adonis, he found plenty when challenged from the second last by Bombyx, pulling clear on the run-in to beat that rival by four and a half lengths.

The fact Paso Doble didn't open his account until after the end of the latest season ensures that he remains a novice over hurdles for the 2021/22 campaign. He has already shown a fairly useful level of form and the experience he gained during the spring is sure to stand him in good stead. It's worth reiterating that longer trips won't hold any fears for him and he appeals as the type to make hay in early-season novice hurdles, with a race such as the Persian War at Chepstow likely to feature on his agenda. *Paul Nicholls*

Conclusion: *Created a good impression in two starts over hurdles to date and has the potential to develop into a smart novice at around 2½m in 2021/22*

Dan Barber (Paso Doble): *"Despite his background on the Flat, and indeed his name, Paso Doble is more about staying power than a quick step, but he waltzed to success at Kempton on his second outing as a novice (having been placed in the Adonis on his first go) and can only progress as his stamina is drawn out this season."*

Pay The Piper (Ire)   h140p

6 b.g. Court Cave (Ire) – Regal Holly (Gildoran)
2020/21 h17v* h17s* h16d* h16d² Mar 20

Ann Hamilton has shown that she knows what to do when she gets a good horse through her hands. Just look at the exploits of the very smart chaser Nuts Well and the useful hurdler Tommy's Oscar, who have racked up 15 wins (and counting) for the yard between them. It's a remarkable story as Hamilton trains only a handful of horses alongside husband Ian and the racing operation is run alongside their main cattle and sheep business.

Hamilton achieved a personal-best tally of 12 winners during the latest season. Nuts Well provided the yard with its biggest success yet when winning the Old Roan Chase at Aintree, while Tommy's Oscar recorded four wins before signing off with a career-best effort to finish third in the Scottish Champion Hurdle at Ayr. Tommy's Oscar wasn't even the highest-rated hurdler in the yard by the end of the campaign, though, with that honour instead falling to Pay The Piper.

A point winner in Ireland, Pay The Piper made a successful debut for Hamilton in a maiden hurdle at Sedgefield in December, hitting the front passing the last and keeping going well to beat Word Has It (who won his next two starts) by three and three quarter lengths. Pay The Piper didn't need to improve on that effort to defy a penalty in a novice hurdle at Carlisle in February, digging deep to get the verdict by a nose, and he then overcame a sloppy round of jumping to complete a hat-trick on his handicap debut at Wetherby the following month, once again showing an excellent attitude as he edged ahead close home to win by a neck.

Pay The Piper lost his unbeaten record under Rules on his final outing at Newcastle in March, but he still showed improved form in defeat and probably would have won with a more fluent jump at the last, ultimately passing the post just a neck behind the winner. He could do with brushing up on his jumping but still has the look of a well-handicapped horse having gone up just 3 lb to a BHA mark of 140 ahead of the 2021/22 campaign. He remains with potential, too, especially as there's longer trips still to explore.
Ann Hamilton

Conclusion: *Came a long way in a short space of time during the latest season and likely to progress further over hurdles; looks capable of winning more handicaps at up to 2½m*

Pounding Poet (Ire)   h126p

5 b.g. Yeats (Ire) – Pestal And Mortar (Ire) (Tamayaz (Can))
2020/21 F16d² h20s⁶ h16d h16v⁴ h20d* :: 2021/22 h21v* May 8

Pounding Poet started his career with Dai Burchell, finishing second in a Uttoxeter bumper in August 2020, before joining the Tom Lacey yard. It was a case of baby steps in the early days with Lacey, running in three novice hurdles between October and December, faring best when fourth at Wetherby on the last occasion. The most encouraging aspect of that performance was the way stayed on gradually in the straight and, upped to 2½m for his handicap debut at Southwell in March, he duly proved a totally different proposition.

Reappearing after 12 weeks on the sidelines, Pounding Poet showed much improved form to get off the mark at Southwell, with the way the race developed helping to mask his superiority. Waited with in the early stages, he travelled powerfully through the race before being forced to wait for a gap leaving the back straight. He tried for a run up the inner early in the straight, but there wasn't enough room to get back inside the wing of the second last, giving his jockey Robert Dunne little choice but to take back. It was hard not to be impressed by the way Pounding Poet put the race to bed once finally getting daylight on the run-in, though, ultimately winning by half a length with plenty up his sleeve.

Pounding Poet had a 6 lb higher mark to contend with when making his next appearance at Warwick in May, but this time he was even more impressive under a ride of rare confidence from Dunne. Once again, the race wasn't without its scares, needing to sit and suffer when short of room before the last, but Pounding Poet was going so well that it made little difference and he breezed to the front under his motionless rider once getting a gap on the run-in, only winning by three quarters of a length but looking value for much more.

Pounding Poet will begin the 2021/22 campaign on a BHA mark of 124, 8 lb higher than when successful at Warwick, and there is little doubt he remains at the right end of the handicap. He is still eligible for low-grade affairs to start with before connections plot the route forward, with the potential there for him to climb a good way up the ladder in the coming months. *Tom Lacey*

Conclusion: *Unbeaten since making the switch to handicaps over hurdles and the style of his last win suggests a BHA mark of 124 is still workable; remains open to more improvement and very much one to keep on the right side*

Rainyday Woman   b106

6 b.m. Kayf Tara – Wistow (Sir Harry Lewis (USA))
2020/21 F16d* F16v* F16v Mar 13

Rainyday Woman takes her name from the Bob Dylan song which reached the top 10 in the UK and US and, while she has some way to go to reach a similar chart position, there was no denying the promise of her first season with Paul Nicholls.

Rainyday Woman began her career with Pam Sly, hitting the frame in bumpers at Market Rasen and Ludlow before wind surgery and a switch to Ditcheat. The new team hit the ground running with her at Stratford in November as she showed improved form in a first-time tongue strap to beat Harde Fashion by nine lengths. Going to the front down the back straight, she quickened clear a furlong out and won in the style of a horse going places. Next stop was Huntingdon for a listed mares' bumper in December and this time Rainyday Woman looked something out of the ordinary. Sent off joint favourite in a field stacked with previous winners, she never looked like being beaten, going on early in the straight and pulling three and a half lengths clear of Flirtatious Girl.

Such was the impression Rainyday Woman created at Huntingdon, she was then sent off the 5/4 favourite for another listed mares' bumper at Sandown in March despite having to concede weight to all round. In the event, the race didn't work out for Rainyday Woman, who was beaten two furlongs out after failing to settle in the testing conditions, but her form still received a boost as the horse she beat at Huntingdon, Flirtatious Girl, ran away with the spoils by two and a quarter lengths.

Hopefully, that was just a blip in Rainyday Woman's progress and her earlier form obviously suggests she can make an impression over jumps in time, with a novice hurdling campaign against her own sex surely on the cards in 2021/22. A really imposing type of mare, she should take well to that discipline, with a step up to 2½m+ likely to play to her strengths judged on her stamina-laden pedigree. ***Paul Nicholls***

Conclusion: *Useful bumper mare who has all the attributes to suggest she can take high rank in the mares' novice hurdling division in 2021/22; will be suited by at least 2½m*

Remastered   c148

8 ch.g. Network (Ger) – Cathodine Cayras (Fr) (Martaline)
2020/21 c20s* c24v* c24s* c30d⁵ Mar 16

Owners Brocade Racing have had a golden few years in staying chases thanks to their flagbearer, Native River, who won a Hennessy (when it was still a Hennessy) and a Welsh National on his way to Cheltenham Gold Cup glory in 2018. Blessed in the stamina department, his relentless style won over the hearts of many a National Hunt racing fan and ensured that the red and blue quartered silks with yellow sleeves will forever be associated with the hard as nails Gold Cup winner.

Having won the Reynoldstown Novices' Chase at Ascot in February, David Pipe's Remastered, under the same ownership, goes into the 2021/22 campaign with a similar profile to the one Native River had ahead of his second season over fences. Indeed, races like the Ladbrokes Trophy and Welsh National are likely to be on Remastered's radar in the upcoming campaign, as he looks a strong stayer with all the right attributes to succeed in those types of contest.

Deep winter ground could well be important to Remastered, as he progressed in heavy conditions and that career-high at Ascot came on soft ground, with his one and only slightly disappointing run over fences last season coming in the National Hunt Chase on good to soft ground at the Cheltenham Festival. Outpaced that day, he came home in a 23-length fifth, but the positive is that he begins his second season over fences from a BHA mark of 146, which looks an attractive one with races like the Newbury highlight in mind.

Whether Remastered can make up into a horse better than a handicapper remains to be seen, but he enters the new season as one of the most exciting staying chasers to emerge from Pond House for a number of years. **David Pipe**

Conclusion: *Made a fine impression as a novice and looks one to keep on the right side in the big staying handicap chases, particularly when the mud is flying*

Rose of Arcadia (Ire)   h114

6 b.m. Arcadio (Ger) – Rosie Lea (Ire) (Supreme Leader)
2020/21 h16d⁴ h15s² h21v* h21d⁵ Mar 27

Sporting the familiar colours of Cheveley Park Stud, Rose of Arcadia shaped like a young horse with a future during the latest season, especially as she did her winning when the Tizzard stable was under a cloud.

After a barren January, Rose of Arcadia ended a losing sequence of 49 runners for the yard when she won a mares' novice hurdle at Wincanton in February, where she just held on in a frantic finish with Nicky Henderson's Fable, having travelled through the race like she would win much more comfortably.

Quicker ground could've been the main factor as to why Rose of Arcadia was outpaced in fifth in the EBF "National Hunt" Novices' Mares' Hurdle at Newbury on her final outing in March, but she again travelled well to the second last and looks worth following now she's got her novice campaign under her belt. The mares' programme ensures Rose of Arcadia will have plenty of opportunities in handicap hurdles at trips around 2½m and that distance on proper winter ground could prove to be her optimum conditions.

An Irish point winner, Rose of Arcadia is the second foal out of Rosie Lea, a half-sister to chase winners Strollawaynow and Lacken Bridge, from the family of Hennessy winner Suny Bay. **Joe Tizzard**

Conclusion: *Will make a chaser in time but should hold her own in handicap hurdles against her own sex in 2021/22; BHA mark of 120 looks far from insurmountable*

Salty Boy (Ire)   c124

8 b.g. Stowaway – Ballons Oscar (Ire) (Oscar (Ire))

2020/21 c20g⁴ c24d⁶ c26v³ c28s⁶ c33s³ Feb 27

David Bridgwater had some terrible luck at the start of 2021 when his best steeplechaser, The Conditional, was fatally injured at Newbury. Twice placed in the Ladbrokes Trophy and a winner at the Cheltenham Festival, The Conditional progressed through the handicap ranks from a lowly beginning and there will be high hopes Salty Boy can do the same.

Like The Conditional, Salty Bay came from Ireland, though he failed to make the immediate impression his stablemate did. His progress has been slow and he's winless from five for his new yard, but there have been clear indications that he's a project that could catch fire in the upcoming campaign granted the right set of circumstances. His best runs during the latest season came behind Sam's Adventure at Haydock and Newcastle, his performance at the latter track in the Eider Chase suggesting that no test of stamina will be too taxing for such a dour stayer. Indeed, he was outpaced in that contest staged over 33f but rallied approaching two out from where he stayed on for an 11-length third.

So, what are the circumstances that look a positive for this horse? Deep ground and a trip look a pre-requisite, while a switch in tactics which sees him dominate from the front end could well be a catalyst for further improvement, too. He certainly looks handicapped to win from a BHA mark of 123—a rating 10 lb lower than his current hurdles mark—so watch out for him in the deep mid-winter staying chases when the mud is flying.

David Bridgwater

Conclusion: *Offered plenty to work on during his first season for this yard and looks handicapped to be competitive in handicap chases where the emphasis is on stamina*

Phil Turner (Salty Boy): *"David Bridgwater endured a torrid time of things in 2020/21 with his lowest wins tally in 11 seasons and, worst of all, the loss of stable star The Conditional through a freak injury at Newbury. The indomitable trainer has regularly shown he can deliver the goods with the right material, though, and Salty Boy appeals as the type he'll do well with this winter. The eight-year-old gelding may still be without a win in five starts for current connections, but his placed efforts in the Tommy Whittle and Eider Chases suggests it won't take long for him to defy a BHA mark in the mid-120s—indeed, like fellow Irish import The Conditional, it wouldn't be a surprise to see him keep on improving the more he tackles good staying handicap company."*

Sam Barton   h127p

6 b.g. Black Sam Bellamy (Ire) – Bartons Bride (Ire) (Anshan)
2020/21 h19d⁵ h20s² h19s* h20v⁴ Mar 13

The yellow, green and white colours of legendary owner Trevor Hemmings will be seen less frequently on the racetrack in 2021/22. The three-time Grand National-winning owner has scaled down the size of his racing interests after four decades in the sport, the 86-year-old citing the impact of Covid-19 as a major factor in his decision. That's the bad news. But the good news is the billionaire owner will continue to have horses on a much smaller scale and, after sending around 50 to the Goffs UK September Sale last year, you can be sure he's kept one or two very nice prospects among his current string.

Step forward Sam Barton, a horse who may as well have had "I'm a chaser" lit up in the illuminations that swung on the streets below Hemmings' Blackpool Tower such is his potential over the bigger obstacles. Built in the mould of many an exciting prospect owned by Hemmings, Sam Barton shaped with bundles of promise in his novice hurdling season in 2020/21. After two educational runs at Chepstow and Hereford in the early months of that campaign, he burst onto the scene with an impressive victory at Doncaster in January, beating three horses in The Edgar Wallace, Up For Parol and Style It Out who subsequently won five races between them.

Sent off 8/1 for the EBF Final at Sandown in March on the back of that, Sam Barton finished fourth on his handicap debut from a BHA mark of 132, shaping very much like a future chaser for a trainer in Emma Lavelle who excels with this type of horse. Her work with De Rasher Counter is the best example of that, while Hemmings has also used the EBF Final as a launchpad for a promising steeplechaser before—a certain Many Clouds was second at Sandown before a glorious chasing career that included Grand National glory.

Sam Barton has a long way to go before he is worthy of being included in discussions with such company, but he's a big, strong gelding with enormous potential and he's expected to climb high in the novice chasing division in 2021/22. *Emma Lavelle*

Conclusion: *Goes into his novice chasing campaign on the back of an educational season over timber and looks built for the job for top connections; will stay 3m*

Ben Linfoot (Sam Barton): *"I really like the look of this fellow for the Emma Lavelle team. The EBF Final has been a breeding ground for some very good steeplechasers including for Sam Barton's owner, Trevor Hemmings, who ran Many Clouds in the Sandown race before he embarked on a stellar fencing career that included Grand National glory. Sam Barton is a lovely-looking strong son of Black Sam Bellamy who ran fourth in the EBF Final on his handicap hurdling debut, shaping every inch like a future chaser. Hopefully he can have a fruitful novice chasing campaign."*

Secret Reprieve (right) wins the Welsh National in impressive fashion

Secret Reprieve (Ire)   c145p

7 b.g. Flemensfirth (USA) – Oscar's Reprieve (Ire) (Oscar (Ire))
2020/21 c26s^F c24s* c31d* Jan 9

William and Angela Rucker's blue silks with pink band were carried around the Grand National course in the big one for four consecutive years by State of Play between 2009 and 2012. In his first three goes he kept on for a share of the prize money, finishing fourth twice and third once under Paul Moloney, albeit he never looked like etching his name on the winners' board. After gaining popularity for his reliability in the famous race, the owners would be forgiven for trying to find the next State of Play. Perhaps they found him with Alvarado, who finished fourth in consecutive Nationals under Moloney in 2014 and 2015, but he hunted round for place money and didn't look like taking the next step which would be Grand National glory.

To be a contender for that you need gears of the kind that both State of Play and Alvarado, for all their heart, were lacking, but in their up-and-coming star chaser Secret Reprieve, the Ruckers may finally have found a horse that could deliver them Aintree glory. Indeed, it could've been last season but for a late twist of fate that saw him miss out on the final field by two, as he was second reserve for the Aintree showpiece before the deadline came with no horses withdrawn.

As short as 12/1 to triumph on Merseyside, the youngster was well fancied after hosing up in the rearranged Welsh Grand National at Chepstow in January, a race he was 8 lb well-in for after winning the trial in stylish fashion a month previously. He won the main event despite adversity, however, as his breast girth became loose three out which could've caused problems for Adam Wedge. As it was, his jockey dealt with the situation coolly, steering him home for a comfortable three-length success.

Secret Reprieve is a strong stayer who jumps soundly and travels well, suggesting he possesses all the necessary attributes for a Grand National. **Evan Williams**

Conclusion: *Missed out on the National last season but is likely to be aimed at that race this time around and has all the potential to be a leading player*

Shallwehaveonemore (Fr) b109p
4 b.g. Authorized (Ire) – Princess Roseburg (USA) (Johannesburg (USA))
2020/21 F16d* Mar 20

Owner Steve Packham knows all too well about the ups and downs of racehorse ownership but clearly the answer to the question posed in the name of the latest horse to carry his white and red colours was a resounding 'Yes!'

Goshen has won seven races on the Flat and over hurdles for Packham and his wide-margin success in the Kingwell Hurdle last February raised hopes that the Champion Hurdle would provide the very smart hurdler with an opportunity to compensate for his infamous unseat at the last at the Cheltenham Festival 12 months earlier when looking to have the Triumph Hurdle sewn up.

It wasn't to be for Goshen in the Champion Hurdle, either, but just four days after that disappointment at Cheltenham, stablemate Shallwehaveonemore must have lifted his owner's mood by making a winning debut in a bumper at Kempton which marked him out as an exciting prospect. Nicky Henderson fielded the favourite, Walking On Air, in a race he had won five times in the last eight runnings, notably with Shishkin in 2019. But Shallwehaveonemore showed more speed and know-how than the favourite who was also making his debut. Patiently ridden and travelling well, Shallwehaveonemore quickened to lead over a furlong out and was soon in command, pulling four and a half lengths clear of Walking On Air who himself finished ten lengths clear of the third.

Not only is Shallwehaveonemore a French-bred, like Goshen, the pair also share the same sire, Authorized, the 2007 Derby winner being best known in jumping circles as the sire of dual Grand National winner Tiger Roll. But Shallwehaveonmore actually has more of a Flat pedigree. His two winning siblings are both Flat winners, though one of them, Asknotwhat, showed some ability over hurdles, while his dam Princess Roseburg was a useful performer at up to 1m for Jean-Claude Rouget in France where she was placed in listed contests. His pedigree, as well as the speed he showed at Kempton, suggests that

Shallwehaveonemore will prove best at 2m, at least for the time being, and he looks sure to do well in novice hurdles. **Gary Moore**

Conclusion: *Impressive winner of a Kempton bumper that had been won by Shishkin, and looks another exciting prospect for the connections of very smart hurdler Goshen*

Shan Blue (Ire)   c150+

7 b.g. Shantou (USA) – Lady Roberta (Ire) (Bob Back (USA))
2020/21 c19g* c24d* c24d* c20v² c20d⁵ c25d² Apr 9

In contrast to his stablemates Allmankind and Protektorat who both ended their first seasons over fences on a high, another of Dan Skelton's leading novices Shan Blue met with a couple of heavy defeats at Cheltenham and Aintree in the spring. But we're confident that he's better than he was able to show on those last two starts and, starting afresh, he seems sure to win more good races in his second season over fences.

Winning pointer Shan Blue had always looked the type to make a better chaser than he was a hurdler and he duly made a perfect start to his chasing career when winning a couple of novices at Wetherby in October by a combined total of 30 lengths. Shan

Shan Blue (left) showed smart form over fences as a novice

Blue really impressed in the jumping department and that proved a huge asset again when he completed his hat-trick in the Kauto Star Novices' Chase at Kempton on Boxing Day. Forcing the pace this time, Shan Blue went harder than ideal in front (he recorded a quicker time than Frodon in the King George that followed) but it was his superior jumping in the closing stages which enabled him to hold on for a three and three-quarter length victory over the less-fluent The Big Breakaway.

Despite winning his last two races over 3m, Shan Blue shaped as though shorter trips might suit him ideally and he appeared next over 2½m in the Scilly Isles Novices' Chase at Sandown with the aim of contesting the Marsh Novices' Chase over the same trip at the Cheltenham Festival. Shan Blue ran close to his best form at Sandown, though on easily the most testing ground he's faced over fences he couldn't see off the late challenge of outsider Sporting John. At Cheltenham, Shan Blue's chances seemed to improve after the early departure of hot favourite Envoi Allen but if Harry Skelton could have the ride again he probably wouldn't press on as early as he did. Shan Blue had a hard race in finishing only fifth behind Chantry House and he probably hadn't fully recovered when a remote second to the same rival in the Mildmay Novices' Chase at Aintree back over a longer trip. The Paddy Power Gold Cup might be a good starting point for Shan Blue in the new season. *Dan Skelton*

Conclusion: *Smart chaser who is best judged on his performances earlier last season when teaching his rivals some jumping lessons*

Small Present (Ire) h128

6 b.g. Presenting – Serpentaria (Golden Snake (USA))
2020/21 h16s² h17g² h20d² h22g⁴ h21v⁴ h25v* h24g* h24m* Apr 3

Mrs Aafke Clarke has had some good jumpers with Sue Smith, none better than the 2018 Scottish Champion Hurdle winner Midnight Shadow who went on to bag two big wins at Cheltenham in the Relkeel Hurdle and Dipper Novices' Chase. Small Present isn't at that level yet himself, but he was really thriving over hurdles by the end of last season and appeals as the type to do well again in 2021/22 in novice chases.

Small Present took a while to get his head in front last season after finishing runner-up on his first three starts of the campaign but the turning point came in a handicap at Catterick in February when he was stepped up in trip. He saw out the 3m1f in testing conditions really well, getting the better of Big Penny by a head as the pair of them pulled clear. Small Present then followed up at Doncaster by half a length from Skandiburg, the first two again a long way clear of the rest, and he completed his hat-trick in a competitive final of the Challenger Stayers Hurdle Series at Haydock in April. From a 12 lb higher mark than at Catterick, Small Present progressed again and stayed on to lead on the line and win by a nose from Colonial Dreams.

The going was good to firm at Haydock, in contrast to the heavy ground he encountered at Catterick, so Small Present is versatile when it comes to underfoot conditions, though it's clearly the step up to 3m or more which brought about the improvement he showed at the end of last season. That's very much in keeping with his breeding as his dam Serpentaria, who was out of a half-sister to the Ascot Gold Cup winner Celeric, showed useful form over hurdles during her time with Willie Mullins, winning at up to 3m herself.

After a largely quiet season, Small Present's form towards the end of the campaign was indicative of a general revival in fortunes for Sue Smith's yard in the spring—Vintage Clouds' victory at the fifth attempt in the Ultima Handicap Chase at the Cheltenham Festival was further evidence of that—and he's one to follow in staying novice chases in the North. **Sue Smith**

Conclusion: *Ended his season with a hat-trick in staying handicap hurdles and he should make a cracking novice chaser given similar tests over fences*

Stage Star (Ire)   b115

5 b.g. Fame And Glory – Sparky May (Midnight Legend)
2020/21 F16s* F16s² F17d³ Apr 10

Readers may recall Sparky May, a mare whose rags-to-riches progress as a novice hurdler in 2010/11 made her one of the stories of that season. Described by her veteran trainer Pat Rodford as 'a freak' on account of her humble breeding- her American dam had apparently been bought with the intention of breeding showjumpers from her—Sparky May won her first four starts over hurdles for her small Somerset stable before having her unbeaten record ended only by Quevega, who was winning the third of her six Mares' Hurdles at the Cheltenham Festival.

Modestly bred or not, Sparky May's ability means she's visited some top National Hunt stallions at stud and she got off the mark as a broodmare when her third foal, Stage Star, by Irish Derby and Ascot Gold Cup winner Fame And Glory, made an impressive winning debut by seven lengths in a bumper at Chepstow last October. That led to Stage Star starting favourite against five other last-time-out winners in a listed bumper at Ascot just before Christmas but he found Paul Nicholls' other runner Knappers Hill a length too good after showing signs of inexperience in his finishing effort. It was April before the pair were seen out again in the Grade 2 bumper at Aintree. While Knappers Hill showed improved form to complete a hat-trick, Stage Star also ran his best race after leading for much of the home straight, finishing clear of the rest in third, a length and three-quarters behind the winner, with Peking Rose, who had finished fourth behind them at Ascot, splitting the Nicholls pair in second.

Stage Star, who had cost €60,000 as a three-year-old, is a rangy gelding who was the pick on looks in the field at Ascot and gave the impression at Aintree that he's at least as good a prospect as the pair who beat him there. He's bred to stay well when he goes over hurdles as Sparky May won up to 3m herself, and his dam's other runner in the latest season, Lanspark, was much improved when successfully stepping up to that trip at Taunton in March. **Paul Nicholls**

Conclusion: *Son of useful mare Sparky May who showed smart form in bumpers and very much the type on looks to prove just as good over hurdles*

St Barts (Ire)   c136

7 b.g. High Chaparral (Ire) – Lindeman (Ire) (Presenting)
2020/21 c24d² c23s* c24s⁵ Mar 20

Owner Richard Kelvin-Hughes came within a neck of realising his dream of breeding a Gold Cup winner when Santini just failed to overhaul Al Boum Photo at Cheltenham in 2020. Perhaps he'll have better luck in the Gold Cup in another season or two with My Drogo, another one of our *Fifty*, who looks to have huge potential over fences. Another homebred in the grey colours with the white epaulets, St Barts might not be a Gold Cup contender himself—for all that he's related to a winner of the race as his dam is out of a half-sister to Denman—but we do see him as a profitable horse to follow this season in staying handicap chases.

St Barts won the first of his two starts in points before joining Philip Hobbs for a hurdling campaign in 2019/20. From just four starts he won twice, a maiden at Uttoxeter and a handicap at Ascot, both races run on heavy ground, and he was well backed for his handicap debut at Ascot when stepping up to nearly 3m for the first time.

St Barts was switched to fences last season and again showed plenty of promise in another light campaign, appearing just three times in novice handicap chases, all at around 3m. He bettered his hurdling form straight away over fences and there was plenty to like about his chasing debut when finishing second to Ofalltheginjoints at Exeter. He duly went one better next time at Newbury in December when making all, jumping well in the main and idling in the closing stages on the way to beating Versatility by two and a quarter lengths. It was then more than three months before St Barts was seen out again and his jumping looked rusty when sent off favourite but finishing only fifth at Uttoxeter on the Midlands National card. It's a race which tends to throw up smart handicappers—Ladbrokes Trophy winner De Rasher Counter won it in 2019 while St Barts' stable has gone close to winning it in the past with Rock The Kasbah. Still with few miles on the clock, St Barts is likely to stay further than 3m and has done all his racing on ground softer than good (acts on heavy). ***Philip Hobbs***

Conclusion: *Lightly-raced staying type who can be forgiven his last run and remains with potential in long-distance handicaps*

Follow us on Twitter @Timeform

Tea Clipper (Ire) h140

6 b.g. Stowaway – A Plus Ma Puce (Fr) (Turgeon (USA))
2020/21 h19m* h21g⁵ F16s⁵ h21d³ h25d³ Apr 10

Monkfish, Put The Kettle On and The Shunter have more in common than all being winners over fences at the 2021 Cheltenham Festival. They're also all by Stowaway who could well have an exciting novice chaser for the coming season in the form of Tea Clipper. He's certainly got the physique for fences, being a tall, close-coupled gelding, and he won his only start in points before making an excellent start over the smaller obstacles, winning four of his first five races over hurdles.

The last of those wins came on Tea Clipper's reappearance last season in the Silver Trophy Handicap Hurdle at Chepstow. Returning from eight months off, he picked up where he left off as a progressive novice the previous season in what was a tougher handicap, impressing most with his response off the bridle. The omission of the final flight resulted in a long run-in, but, having led around two furlongs out, Tea Clipper found plenty and saw off final challenger Flash The Steel inside the final furlong to win going away by two and a quarter lengths.

While Tea Clipper failed to add to that success in the remainder of the season, he proved better than ever when picking up place money on his last couple of starts at Cheltenham and Aintree in the spring. He outran his odds of 33/1 to take third behind Heaven Help Us and Craigneiche in the Coral Cup at Cheltenham, running on after being hampered at the last, before faring better still when stepping up to 3m for the first time in another competitive Grade 3 handicap at Aintree. With Rachael Blackmore in the saddle this time, replacing regular jockey Jonathan Burke who was on another of the leading contenders Come On Teddy, Tea Clipper briefly disputed second after jumping the final flight before finishing third behind Hometown Boy and J'Ai Froid, beaten just under eight lengths behind the winner. Effective on soft and good to firm ground, there's every reason to think Tea Clipper will do at least as well over fences. ***Tom Lacey***

Conclusion: *Smashing novice chase prospect after ending last season with third places in competitive handicap hurdles at Cheltenham and Aintree*

The Ferry Master (Ire) c136p

8 b.g. Elusive Pimpernel (USA) – Dinghy (Ire) (Be My Native (USA))
2020/21 c20s² c23d* c23g* c20v⁴ c32g⁴ Apr 18

Sandy Thomson, who trains not far from Kelso in the Scottish Borders, enjoyed his best season yet in 2020/21, with 29 winners, while the stable's total prize money of more than £340,000 was surpassed only by Donald McCain and Lucinda Russell among yards in the North. A fine advert for the stable was Yorkhill's win at 66/1 in the Rehearsal Chase at Newcastle in November on just his second outing for Thomson, Yorkhill having won only once for Willie Mullins since his Cheltenham Festival success in 2017. Another old chaser sweetened up by the yard was Seeyouatmidnight who gained his second success since coming out of retirement when winning the valuable final of the Veterans' Series at Sandown just days after turning 13.

Seeyouatmidnight finished third in a Scottish Grand National as a novice and stablemate The Ferry Master, a novice himself, ran an excellent race to finish fourth in the latest renewal of that race at Ayr. The stable was also represented by runner-up Dingo Dollar, another revived by the switch to Thomson, but it was The Ferry Master who shaped best of all, looming up as if the likely winner on the home turn but unable to master Dingo Dollar three out and then run out of the placings as another novice, Mighty Thunder, went on to win. The Ferry Master shaped like an old hand at Ayr, jumping and travelling really well before just coming up short on stamina on his first try at such an extreme trip.

The Ferry Master had looked nothing out of the ordinary over hurdles the previous season when he had needed the help of the stewards to grant him victory in a three-runner contest at Carlisle but he progressed really well over fences and won novice handicaps at Kelso and Newcastle in November. He's one to keep on side in the good staying chases in the North this season, with the Scottish Borders National at Kelso in December, a race his stable has won four times since 2014, a likely target in the first part of the season. He's certainly worth another try over an extreme trip, and there's further improvement to come from him. **Sandy Thomson**

Conclusion: *Went like the best horse when fourth in the Scottish Grand National as a novice and looks a staying chaser to follow for a stable that does well with such types*

Third Time Lucki (Ire)   h143

6 br.g. Arcadio (Ger) – Definite Valley (Ire) (Definite Article)
2020/21 h16d* h16d* h16v² h16d* h16d⁴ h17d⁶ h16d⁴ Apr 9

Such was the domination of the Irish at Cheltenham that few British-trained runners returned a single-figure SP in any of the Festival's handicaps, but an exception was Third Time Lucki in the County Hurdle. It's a race Third Time Lucki's trainer Dan Skelton has won three times since 2016 so he was entitled to plenty of respect on his first start outside novice company. He gave a good account too, but went for home a bit too soon entering the straight, being collared approaching the last and then cracking late on after a brief rally put him back in front on the run-in. Even so, Third Time Lucki shaped as though ahead of his mark in sixth as the more patiently-ridden Belfast Banter held off Petit Mouchoir in an Irish-trained one-two.

Third Time Lucki had to give Belfast Banter a stone at Cheltenham but he failed to take advantage of meeting that rival on level terms in the Top Novices' Hurdle at Aintree and could finish only fourth in a race which again went to Belfast Banter. Third Time Lucki's first season over hurdles may have ended with a rather flat effort, but he had a largely progressive profile prior to Cheltenham, winning at Uttoxeter, Wetherby and Kempton. Some talented horses have won the Kempton race he landed on Boxing Day, including Altior, and Third Time Lucki took it in good style by nine lengths from Flic Ou Voyou. His County Hurdle effort was the second time that he has run well at the Festival, coming 12 months after his fourth place behind Ferny Hollow and Appreciate It in the Champion Bumper.

The angular Third Time Lucki was second on his only start in Irish points before his bumper campaign in Britain so will presumably be sent over fences this season. A strong traveller who has raced only at around 2m, he should take high rank among the novices over that trip, perhaps going for some of the same races which stablemate Allmankind did so well in last season. **Dan Skelton**

Conclusion: *Showed useful form in his first season over hurdles, shaping well in the County Hurdle, and looks the type to prove at least as good in 2m novice chases*

Thyme Hill h158

7 b.g. Kayf Tara – Rosita Bay (Hernando (Fr))
2020/21 h24g* h24s² h25d* Apr 10

Thyme Hill was this publication's ante-post tip for the Stayers' Hurdle last season and all seemed to be going to plan until the week before Cheltenham when a pulled muscle ruled him out of the race. That was hard luck for anyone who'd supported him for Cheltenham, but happily it was only a minor setback in the wider scheme of things, and

Thyme Hill (left) looks a leading contender for the 2022 Stayers' Hurdle

his subsequent success when favourite for the Liverpool Hurdle just weeks later showed that he'll be the one to beat among Britain's top staying hurdlers in the coming season when hopefully he'll make it to Cheltenham this time.

Thyme Hill had a new jockey at Aintree, with Tom O'Brien bringing him with a perfectly timed run to beat the mare Roksana by a neck. O'Brien had also ridden Thyme Hill for his debut win in a Worcester bumper but all his subsequent outings had been for four-time champion Richard Johnson, who had announced his shock retirement from the saddle at Newton Abbot just a week before Aintree. Johnson's final success aboard Thyme Hill had come at Newbury in November when weight and fitness had helped him get the better of former Stayers' Hurdle winner Paisley Park in the Long Distance Hurdle. The pair met again in the Long Walk Hurdle at Ascot the following month when Thyme Hill looked to have the race won only to idle in front as Paisley Park mowed him down in the shadow of the post for a neck win. That whetted the appetite for further clashes between the two of them but it wasn't to be. When they did eventually meet again, in the Liverpool Hurdle, Paisley Park ran poorly after finishing third to the Irish pair Flooring Porter and Sire du Berlais when trying to win the Stayers' again, suggesting that the main hopes of keeping that prize at home next March now lie principally with the younger Thyme Hill. The programme for the top staying hurdlers is well established, and no doubt it will be Newbury and Ascot again before Christmas for Thyme Hill, with perhaps the Cleeve Hurdle an option in the New Year before the Cheltenham Festival and Aintree again. **Philip Hobbs**

Conclusion: *Ended the season with strong claims to being Britain's top staying hurdler and will hopefully get a crack at the Stayers' Hurdle this season*

Time To Get Up (Ire)   c143p

8 ch.g. Presenting – Gales Return (Ire) (Bob's Return (Ire))
2020/21 c20s^3 c19v^4 c25v* c34s* Mar 20

Minella Times provided J. P. McManus with a second Grand National winner in April after Don't Push It had been his first winner in 2010. Don't Push It also famously provided Sir Anthony McCoy with his only success in the race and changed the Aintree fortunes of his trainer Jonjo O'Neill who had a luckless record in the Grand National as a jockey. McManus and O'Neill could well have another leading contender for the Grand National in 2022 with Time To Get Up, a lightly-raced staying chaser whose Midlands Grand National victory marked him down as a likely type for the Aintree version.

Time To Get Up was in his first season with O'Neill in 2020/21 after just three runs over hurdles in Ireland with Joseph O'Brien, finishing second to Monkfish, no less, in a maiden at Fairyhouse on his final start there. It was almost a year before he had his first start for O'Neill, making an eye-catching debut over fences in finishing third to another of his owner's runners, Canelo, in a novices' handicap at Aintree's November meeting. That was over 2½m, but it was not until Time To Get Up was stepped up to 3m for the first time that he fulfilled that promise, showing plenty of improvement and jumping better than previously to land a competitive handicap at Wincanton in February in comfortable fashion by five lengths from the hat-trick-seeking Shanty Alley.

From an 8 lb higher mark, Time To Get Up looked on a good mark for the following month's Midlands Grand National and he was sent off the 3/1 favourite at Uttoxeter against 19 rivals, most of them much more exposed. A steady gallop ensured plenty were still in contention going to the fourth-last with Mighty Thunder the first to strike for home. However, after conceding first run to Mighty Thunder when untidy three out, Time To Get Up stayed on to lead in the final 50 yards and win by a length. The runner-up gained compensation by winning the Scottish Grand National the following month. With few miles on the clock, there's surely a good deal more to come from Time To Get Up whose campaign will no doubt be geared around a Grand National bid. **Jonjo O'Neill**

Conclusion: *Lightly-raced chaser who improved for greater tests of stamina later in the season and looked an Aintree type when landing the Midlands version at Uttoxeter*

£10 FREE DOWNLOADS AT TIMEFORM.COM

Get free credit to spend when you sign-up

Register a new account with Timeform and we will give you £10 to spend on downloads, tips or subscriptions. No deposit required.

Find out what to spend your free credit on at bit.ly/TFVCode.

You'll bet smarter!

TIMEFORM
PLAY SMARTER

Flags | Ratings | Insight | Analysis

SECTION

2

Appreciate It (Ire) h160p

7.b.g. Jeremy (USA) – Sainte Baronne (Fr) (Saint Des Saints (Fr))
2020/21 h16v* h16s* h16s* h16d* Mar 16

It's fair to say that the 2021 Cheltenham Festival got underway in extraordinary fashion. Not only was the meeting staged behind closed doors due to the Covid-19 pandemic, but the traditional curtain-raiser, the Supreme Novices' Hurdle, also produced a winner of great significance in the shape of Appreciate It, who passed the post with 24 lengths to spare over his nearest rival, the widest winning margin in any race over hurdles at the Festival this century.

It wasn't a surprise to anyone that Appreciate It won the Supreme. After all, he was sent off the 11/8-on favourite after winning his three previous starts over hurdles, including a pair of Grade 1 events at Leopardstown. Nobody could have expected the manner of his Cheltenham success, though, as he put good horses to the sword in relentless fashion after quickening early in the straight. Admittedly, the margin of victory would have been considerably less had stablemate Blue Lord not fallen at the last, but the timefigure provided plenty of substance to the form, suggesting Appreciate It was full

Appreciate It ran out an emphatic winner of the Supreme

value for not just a high-class performance but also the best in the race since Altior in 2016.

Beaten just once since his debut under Rules, in the 2020 Champion Bumper, Appreciate It ended the latest season as Timeform's highest-rated novice hurdler in training, edging out the Ballymore winner Bob Olinger to that honour. A winning pointer, he's a real powerhouse to look at, outstanding even in a good field at Cheltenham, and there is no saying how high he could climb when he embarks on his chasing career in 2021/22. He's bred to stay a good deal further than 2m but seems likely to follow the same path as Altior and attempt to win the Arkle. *Willie Mullins*

Conclusion: *Unbeaten in four starts as a novice hurdler and expected to prove similarly difficult to beat when making the switch to fences; looks tailormade for the Arkle*

Echoes In Rain (Fr)   h151p
5.b.m. Authorized (Ire) – Amarantine (Fr) (King's Best (USA))
2020/21 h16v* h16v⁴ h15s* h16d* :: 2021/22 h16d* Apr 27

Willie Mullins saddled a record-breaking 19 winners at the 2021 Punchestown Festival, a haul which included nine of the 12 Grade 1 races staged at the meeting. Mullins was particularly dominant in the novice hurdling ranks, winning all three top-level contests in that division at Punchestown, a feat he achieved despite Appreciate It, his best novice hurdler, staying tucked up in his box at Closutton.

As previously discussed, Appreciate It looks likely to embark on a chasing career this season, leaving a vacancy for an up-and-comer who might be capable of challenging Honeysuckle's dominance in the 2m hurdling ranks. If there is another horse at Closutton who might be up to the task, then look no further than Echoes In Rain, who made the most of her stablemate's absence at Punchestown to make the breakthrough in Grade 1 company in the 2m Champion Novice Hurdle.

Admittedly, the bare form is probably sub-par for that particular race and Echoes In Rain was more workmanlike than impressive in victory, beating the maiden Colonel Mustard by only three and a quarter lengths. It would be unfair to judge her too harshly on that run, though, especially as it came just three weeks on from a scintillating success in Grade 2 company at Fairyhouse.

Echoes In Rain was burdened with a penalty at Fairyhouse after winning a similar event on her previous start at Naas – when beating the subsequent County Hurdle/ Top Novices' Hurdle winner Belfast Banter by eight lengths – but it made no difference as she quickly spreadeagled the field after getting a gap between the final two flights, ultimately landing the spoils by 15 lengths. The way she shot clear was all the more meritorious given that the pace had been on the slow side and she hadn't settled fully in a tightly-bunched field.

Echoes In Rain, a recruit from the Flat in France, is clearly blessed with plenty of speed, so it will be interesting to see whether she is aimed at the Champion Hurdle or if Mullins feels she can be as effective over 2½m in the Mares' Hurdle. Either way, she remains largely unexposed and should be up to making a serious impact in open graded company. **Willie Mullins**

Conclusion: *Strong-travelling sort who looked a novice out of the very top drawer when winning a Grade 2 at Fairyhouse; remains with potential and doesn't have much to find to develop into a Champion Hurdle contender with the sex allowance*

Energumene (Fr)   c169p
7.br.g. Denham Red (Fr) – Olinight (Fr) (April Night (Fr))
2020/21 c20v* c16v* c17s* :: 2021/22 c16d* Apr 29

Timeform ran a series during the first Covid-19 lockdown reflecting on clashes that all racing fans wanted to see but ultimately never came to fruition. Dubai Millennium vs Montjeu, Motivator vs Shamardal and Cracksman vs Enable all featured, while Big Buck's vs Quevega was the chief example in the recent history of National Hunt racing.

It would be tempting to add Energumene vs Shishkin to that list after the latest season, when the two unbeaten novice chasers were due to meet in the Sporting Life Arkle at the Cheltenham Festival before a late setback ruled Energumene out. All is not lost, though, and there is still every chance we'll get the opportunity to see them square off at some stage this season, a tantalising prospect even before established stars such as Chacun Pour Soi—a stablemate of Energumene—are thrown into the mix.

With a Timeform rating of 171p, Shishkin ended last season as the highest-rated novice chaser in training, but Energumene wasn't far behind after winning all four starts in Ireland by a cumulative margin of around 52 lengths. Energumene didn't come off the bridle in his first three races over fences, which included a 10-length win in the Irish Arkle at Leopardstown, and he saved his best effort for last when winning the Ryanair Novice Chase at the Punchestown Festival. Clearly none the worse for the setback which forced him to miss Cheltenham, Energumene had a couple of very smart rivals in trouble a long way out and proceeded to draw clear in the straight despite untidy jumps at the final two fences, ultimately winning by 16 lengths from Janidil.

Energumene is yet to be truly tested in five starts over obstacles—he easily won his only race over hurdles at Gowran Park in March 2020—and there is almost certainly more to come from him when the situation demands it. He stays 2½m but seems likely to have his campaign geared around a crack at the Champion Chase at the Cheltenham Festival, partly because Chacun Pour Soi failed to take advantage of a golden opportunity to give trainer Willie Mullins a first win in the race in 2021. **Willie Mullins**

Conclusion: *Utterly dominant in four wins from the front as a novice chaser and remains open to more improvement; sure to be challenging the likes of Chacun Pour Soi and Shishkin at the top of the 2m chasing tree*

Gabynako (Fr)   h139

6.b.g. Tirwanako (Fr) – Gunboatfrance (Fr) (Gunboat Diplomacy (Fr))
2020/21 h16s² h16v² h16v* h20v³ h20v³ h16s h20d^ur :: 2021/22 h20d⁵ May 1

Willie Mullins and Henry de Bromhead were the winning-most trainers at the 2021 Cheltenham Festival with six victories apiece, but an honourable mention must also go to Gavin Cromwell, who sent out only five runners at the meeting but struck with Flooring Porter in the Stayers' Hurdle and Vanillier in the Albert Bartlett Novices' Hurdle. There was also plenty of confidence behind Cromwell's Gabynako in the Martin Pipe Conditional Jockeys' Handicap Hurdle, but he was effectively brought down at the first, so we'll never know how he would have fared.

Gavin Cromwell (right) poses with Flooring Porter after the Stayers' Hurdle

He had certainly created a good impression during a busy first campaign over hurdles. Gabynako hit the crossbar on his first two attempts over timber before making the most of a good opportunity to get off the mark in a maiden hurdle at Naas. That performance earned him a step up in grade and he took his form up a notch when placed on his next two starts, finishing third in a Grade 2 at Navan (beaten six and three quarter lengths behind Ashdale Bob) before filling the same position in a Grade 1 back at Naas (beaten eight and three quarter lengths behind Bob Olinger).

Gabynako's first two runs in handicaps didn't exactly go to plan, finishing well held at Leopardstown before his Cheltenham mishap, but he resumed his progress on his final outing at the Punchestown Festival, showing useful form when fifth (beaten five and a half lengths) in another big-field handicap.

Runner-up on his sole start in points, Gabynako is very much the type to make a better chaser. Winning a beginners' chase should prove little more than a formality and, though likely to come up short against the best novice chasers around in Ireland, he will be worth keeping on the right side for a valuable handicap later in the season. **Gavin Cromwell**

Conclusion: *Useful hurdler who has the physique to take well to chasing and could be one for a big handicap at around 2½m*

Journey With Me (Ire)　　　　　　　　b105P

5.ch.g. Mahler – Kilbarry Demon (Ire) (Bob's Return (Ire))
2020/21 F18v* Mar 12

"Could hardly have been more impressive when making a winning bumper debut and looks sure to make his mark over hurdles."

That was the Timeform verdict on Bob Olinger in last year's edition of Horses To Follow. Bob Olinger certainly made his mark—he ended the campaign as one of the highest-rated novice hurdlers in training after an emphatic success in the Ballymore at Cheltenham—and similar comments apply to Journey With Me, who was no less impressive when winning the same Gowran Park bumper for the same set of connections in March.

Successful on his sole outing in points four months earlier, Journey With Me was sent off the 7/4-on favourite to make a winning debut under Rules at Gowran. In truth, anyone who got stuck in at the short odds never really had any cause for concern as Journey With Me produced a dominant display, making light of the extremely demanding conditions. He was always travelling strongly at the head of affairs and had matters well in hand from as far as five furlongs out, not needing to come off the bridle to dish out a 13-length beating to his six rivals.

Just like Bob Olinger before him, Journey With Me was put away after that victory to be readied for a novice hurdling campaign. It's hard to be dogmatic about what his optimum trip will be, but he's likely to be suited by at least 2½m given how well he stayed 2¼m

Journey With Me will be trying to emulate illustrious stablemate Bob Olinger

on heavy going at Gowran. Either way, he must be considered another exciting prospect for the Henry de Bromhead yard which continues to go from strength to strength. **Henry de Bromhead**

Conclusion: *Could hardly have been more impressive when making a winning bumper debut and looks sure to make his mark over hurdles*

Letsbeclearaboutit (Ire)   b114

6.b.g. Flemensfirth (USA) – Clarification (Ire) (Westerner)
2020/21 F16v* F17v* F16v² F16s² F16d* Apr 3

The Willie Mullins-trained pair of Kilcruit (124) and Sir Gerhard (123) achieved the highest ratings in bumpers in 2020/21 and Letsbeclearaboutit had the misfortune of bumping into them both at different times during the latest season. However, he still ran to a useful level in defeat whilst promising plenty for when he gets the opportunity to tackle staying trips over hurdles.

Letsbeclearaboutit made the perfect start to life in bumpers, getting off the mark on his debut at Tipperary by seven lengths from Enniskerry, before showing much improved form to follow up at Punchestown, beating the same rival by eight lengths despite being much worse off at the weights. That success earned Letsbeclearaboutit a step up in grade as he went head-to-head with Sir Gerhard—at that stage trained by Gordon Elliott before moving to Mullins shortly before Cheltenham—in a listed event at Navan. Letsbeclearaboutit was allowed to dictate a modest pace but simply couldn't live with Sir Gerhard's superior change of gear in the final furlong, ultimately passing the post four and a half lengths behind that rival.

Next up for Letsbeclearaboutit was the Grade 2 bumper at Leopardstown's Dublin Racing Festival, a race which was run in very different fashion with the leaders going off far too fast. That played right into the hands of the patiently ridden Kilcruit, who didn't need to come off the bridle to win by 12 lengths, but runner-up Letsbeclearboutit deserves plenty of credit as he emerged as the best of those ridden prominently. Having then bypassed a rematch with Sir Gerhard and Kilcruit at Cheltenham, Letsbeclearaboutit made the most of a good opportunity to end the season with a comfortable win at Fairyhouse, typically travelling well at the head of affairs and just needing to be kept up to his work to beat the useful Harry Alonzo (who received 3 lb) by a length and a half.

Letsbeclearabout held his form well in his five starts in bumpers, giving him an excellent platform to build on with a view to going hurdling. There is plenty of stamina in his pedigree—his grandam is the Champion Stayers Hurdle winner Refinement—and he looks sure to make an impact in the novice hurdling ranks over 2½m+, with the Albert Bartlett, won by stablemate Vanillier in 2021, appealing as a suitable end-of-season target. **Gavin Cromwell**

Conclusion: *Likeable sort who reached a useful level in bumpers and has the potential to climb higher still in novice hurdles over 2½m+*

Mt Leinster Gold (Ire)   h127p

7.b.m. Gold Well – Halfway Home (Presenting)
2020/21 h16v* h24d* :: 2021/22 h21d⁶ Apr 28

Colin Bowe is perhaps best known for nurturing Cheltenham Festival winners such as Envoi Allen and Samcro in their formative years, both impressive point winners for Bowe before being sold for big money to embark on a career under Rules. Bowe is also a successful trainer under Rules in his own right, though, with Askanna, Little King Robin and Shantou Flyer all winning graded races for the yard earlier this century. And, in the shape of Mt Leinster Gold, Bowe looks to have another good prospect to go to war with.

A multiple point winner, Mt Leinster Gold also won her first two starts over hurdles during the latest season, beating mares in a maiden at Fairyhouse before following up in a novice (limited to horses rated up to 116) at Wexford. She only won by three quarters of a length on the last occasion but was almost certainly value for extra, with the steady gallop masking her superiority in a race which has worked out well. Mt Leinster Gold made her final appearance in a conditional jockeys' handicap at the Punchestown Festival, where she shaped much better than the bare result in sixth. Slowly into her stride after a series of false starts, she still had plenty to do three out and stayed on well under the circumstances to be beaten less than 10 lengths, especially as she was hampered after two out and forced wide.

On that evidence, Mt Leinster Gold is almost certainly a well-handicapped horse from a mark of 123. She is every inch a chaser on looks but has unfinished business over hurdles in the meantime, with further improvement on the cards after only three starts. Her strength at the finish at Punchestown suggests she will be suited by a return to 3m and she will have plenty of options, including against her own sex. **Colin Bowe**

Conclusion: *Lightly raced sort who looks on a good mark for handicap hurdles at around 3m; has the background/physique to make a chaser if connections decide on a quick switch, too*

Party Central (Ire) b106

5.b.m. Yeats (Ire) – Itsalark (Ire) (Definite Article)
2020/21 F16d* F16v² F16s² F16d* Apr 3

Noel and Valerie Moran have been huge investors in Irish National Hunt racing over the last couple of seasons and they have plenty to look forward to. They are likely to be particularly strong in the novice hurdling ranks, with a couple of their big-money purchases set to go down that route after showing plenty of promise in bumpers. They include Ginto (cost £398,305), who opened his account at the second attempt at Navan in February, and Hollow Games (cost £255,000), who was unbeaten in two starts before missing the major spring festivals.

The mare Party Central is also one to be excited about having achieved a useful level of form in four starts in bumpers against her own sex. She was bought privately and joined the Gordon Elliott yard after making an impressive winning debut for Roger McGrath in a maiden at Tipperary. She had to settle for second on her next two starts, in a listed event at Navan and a Grade 2 at Leopardstown, but both times she shaped with plenty of encouragement. At Navan she was caught back further than ideal in a steadily-run race, while at Leopardstown she showed improved form to be beaten just a neck behind Grangee despite not getting the clearest of runs.

Party Central didn't need to improve on that effort to resume winning ways on her final outing at Fairyhouse, landing a listed event by a length and three quarters in ready fashion. That victory capped a productive first season and she looks to possess all the tools to make an impact in novice hurdles against mares in 2021/22, with all roads likely to lead to the Dawn Run at the Cheltenham Festival. Incidentally, Party Central is the second horse out of Itsalark to feature in this edition of Horses To Follow. Craigneiche, who showed useful form when filling the runner-up spot in the Coral Cup at the latest Festival, is also one to follow. **Gordon Elliott**

Conclusion: *Showed plenty of ability in bumpers and looks an above-average hurdler in the making; could be an early shout for the Dawn Run at Cheltenham*

Politesse (Ire)   c131p

7.b.m. Beat Hollow – Dalamine (Fr) (Sillery (USA))
2020/21 h16s⁵ h16g⁵ :: 2021/22 h20d⁴ c20s* May 30

Dalamine was a 2m winner on the Flat in France, but it's fair to say that her achievements in the paddocks have far outstripped anything she ever did on a racecourse. She is already the dam of five winners over jumps, a group which includes the smart hurdler/ top-class chaser Don Poli (by Poliglote) and the smart hurdler/useful chaser Debece (by Kayf Tara). In fact, Debece only just missed out on being included in this edition of Horses To Follow having joined Dan Skelton halfway through the latest season, still possessing a very workable mark to exploit in veteran chases.

One horse who should be followed this season is Politesse, a daughter of Dalamine who is already rated higher over fences than she was over hurdles after making a successful start to her chasing career at Punchestown in May. A bumper winner back in March 2020, Politesse was no slouch over hurdles either as she showed fairly useful form in only four starts, producing her best effort on the last of them when beaten around 17 lengths into fourth behind Stormy Ireland in the Mares Champion Hurdle at the Punchestown Festival.

Everything about Politesse, including her rangy physique, pointed to her making further progress over fences, so it was good to see her confirm that impression with an impressive victory on debut. She travelled with plenty of zest at the head of affairs and then cruised clear in the straight to win by 11 lengths, comprehensively seeing off a well-fancied pair from top yards. She jumped slowly at a couple of fences late on but was otherwise very assured for a mare with such little experience.

There is a good programme for mares in Ireland and Politesse looks sure to progress and win more races against her own sex. She has raced mostly at 2m but seemed well suited to 2½m on her final two starts. ***Lorna Fowler***

Conclusion: *Borderline useful hurdler who can be placed to win more races over fences after a dominant debut success at Punchestown in May*

Walk Away (Ire)   c138p

8.b.g. Black Sam Bellamy (Ire) – Pegus Love (Ire) (Executive Perk)
2020/21 c24vᶠ :: 2021/22 c21d² Apr 30

Asterion Forlonge failed to scale the heights expected of him over fences during the first part of the latest season, but he finally put it all together at the Punchestown Festival, showing high-class form to defy top weight on his first foray into handicap company. The official winning margin was 14 lengths and he looks sure to make an impact back in graded races, following in the footsteps of Kemboy (2018) and Real Steel (2019), both of whom won that Punchestown heat for Willie Mullins before going on to taste success at a much higher level.

It's always an informative contest and often it pays to look beyond the obvious when trying to identify promising types. After all, the likes of Tranquil Sea (second in 2009), Golden Silver (fourth in 2009), Road To Riches (second in 2014) and Balko des Flos (third in 2017) have all been beaten in the race this century before going on to win in Grade 1 company later in their careers.

With that in mind, Walk Away could be a horse to keep on the right side after emerging as the best of the rest in the latest edition, proving no match for Asterion Forlonge but still matching the pick of his previous efforts over fences. The form looks even better now than it did at the time—the fifth Fan de Blues and eighth Antey both won next-time-out—and Walk Away could arguably have his effort marked up given that it was just his second run in handicaps and his first since taking a heavy fall in the Munster National at Limerick nearly seven months earlier.

Walk Away is a long way off running in Grade 1 races over fences, but it's surely only a matter of time before he gets off the mark with his novice status intact for 2021/22. That will give him plenty of options and he is still low-mileage for an eight-year-old, so it will be no surprise if he has lots more to offer for his top yard. *Henry de Bromhead*

Conclusion: *Still a maiden after five starts over fences but ended last season with a good second in a valuable novice handicap at the Punchestown Festival; looks a banker for a maiden before going back up in grade*

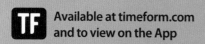

SECTION

TALKING TO THE TRAINERS

We asked a number of leading National Hunt trainers to pick out a chaser, hurdler and novice to follow for the coming season. Here's what they said...

Kim Bailey

Wins-Runs in Britain in 2020/21	**59/313**	
Highest-rated horse in training	**First Flow** Timeform Rating c163	

Chaser: Vinndication (c162): "He's slightly a forgotten horse after two runs over hurdles at the back-end of last season, but his chase form prior to that was very good. He has had back and wind operations this summer and we hope we can get him back on track."

Hurdler: Pipesmoker (h128): "He's new to us this year. He hasn't been easy to train but, if we can keep him sound, he has some very good form in the book and could run in novice hurdles or chases."

Novice: Hamilton Dici (h111): "He won a novice hurdle last season and we think he's worth following in novice handicap chases."

Nicky Henderson

Wins-Runs in Britain in 2020/21	**103/545**	
Highest-rated horse in training	**Shishkin** Timeform Rating c171p	

Chaser: Shishkin (c171p): "We'll start him off in the Tingle Creek at Sandown I would imagine. I hope he can follow in the footsteps of Sprinter Sacre and Altior, but it's going to be a very tough division. If you took Willie Mullins out of the equation, I would say we have a big chance! Come March, the Champion Chase could be the race of the season."

Hurdler: Buzz (h156): "He was very progressive last season and finished second in a Grade 1 at Aintree on his final start. We'll be going up to 3m with him and he might be effective there as long as it's soft ground."

Novice: I Am Maximus (b108): "He should have run again after winning at Cheltenham, but we gave him a break after that first run and we were never going to do too much with him. I'm not a great fan of the Champion Bumper and then the ground dried up and we didn't get another run into him, but I didn't feel that we needed to. He'll be running in novice hurdles somewhere between 2m and 2½m. I think the novice hurdlers might be our strongest division this season."

Philip Hobbs

Wins-Runs in Britain in 2020/21	**54/464**
Highest-rated horse in training	**Defi du Seuil** Timeform Rating c164?

Chaser: Zanza (c143+): "He was very unlucky last season and should continue to progress."

Hurdler: Thyme Hill (h158): "He had a fantastic season and should win more top-class races over hurdles."

Novice: Luttrell Lad (b106): "He had some good bumper form last season. He will start in novice hurdles at 2m but should stay further."

Alan King

Wins-Runs in Britain in 2020/21	**54/405**
Highest-rated horse in training	**Sceau Royal** Timeform Rating c163

Chaser: The Glancing Queen (h126): "She was a top bumper filly and had good graded form over hurdles. She's an Irish point winner and we look forward to going chasing with her. She's a mare we've always liked."

Hurdler: Her Indoors (h126): "She had a good season, winning at Aintree and in a listed race at Cheltenham at the April meeting. She's done really well through the summer and I think she'll improve when we step her up in trip. I hope she'll be good enough to run in those graded mares' hurdles during the winter."

Novice: Haseefah (f86): "She was a winner on the Flat in France and ran well on her last start for me when she was just beaten in a handicap at Goodwood. She'll probably have one more run on the Flat towards the end of September and then go mares' novice hurdling. She's 79-rated at the minute and she's probably better than that. She could be very interesting as she's schooled well."

Donald McCain

Wins-Runs in Britain in 2020/21	**66/486**
Highest-rated horse in training	**Navajo Pass** Timeform Rating h151

Chaser: Gaelik Coast (c134): "He didn't do an awful lot wrong last season and ran well in the Red Rum at Aintree but for a couple of mistakes in the straight. I think he'll be running over a bit further and he'll probably end up jumping the National fences if we can get him in one of those races."

Navajo Pass won the Champion Hurdle Trial at Haydock last season

Hurdler: Navajo Pass (h151): "I think we'll be staying over hurdles with him. We're still not 100% sure of his optimum trip. We dropped back to 2m at Haydock on extreme ground, but we've always been of the opinion that he would get 3m. He proved he's a smart horse last season. It was a year where four-year-olds tend to get lost, but he still managed to win a couple of nice races."

Novice: Dreams of Home (h129p): "He won three novice hurdles at around 2m, but he looks every inch a staying chaser. I've not schooled him over fences yet but, if he goes and schools well and takes to the job, he could be a really nice young National Hunt horse."

Olly Murphy

Wins-Runs in Britain in 2020/21	**80/567**
Highest-rated horse in training	**Itchy Feet** Timeform Rating c154

Chaser: Champagnesuperover (h134): "He was probably never 100% right throughout last season. He ran very well in the Albert Bartlett at Cheltenham and he's summered very well. He's made for jumping fences and could be a horse who progresses massively as a novice chaser."

Hurdler: Thomas Darby (h153): "He stepped up to 3m in the Grade 1 at Aintree on his final start and seemed to show massive improvement. He's going to contest all the good 3m graded races over hurdles and he's hopefully got untapped potential at the trip."

Novice: Go Dante (b110): "He could be a smart novice hurdler. He was a very impressive winner of a bumper for me and his work has always been very good. He jumps like a real smart horse."

Dr Richard Newland

Wins-Runs in Britain in 2020/21	**49/310**	
Highest-rated horse in training	**Captain Tom Cat**	Timeform Rating c148+

Chaser: Enqarde (c129): "He had a very nice first season with us, winning over fences at Ascot, and I'd be hopeful there is more to come. It was probably one race too many in the Scottish National on his final start and I'd like to think there is another decent handicap chase in him."

Hurdler: Benson (h133): "He's a very talented horse but a bit quirky. We've been working hard on his schooling and he's come back in good form. He will be aimed at the decent handicap hurdles and might improve for a step up in trip."

Novice: Doubleubee (h112): "He's a big, strong horse by Yeats who will definitely make a chaser. We only had half a season with him last year and we never got anywhere really. He's due to run fairly shortly, but I think we've definitely not seen the best of him."

Paul Nicholls

Wins-Runs in Britain in 2020/21	**176/705**	
Highest-rated horse in training	**Clan des Obeaux**	Timeform Rating c170

Chaser: Hitman (c152p): "I think he's got huge improvement in him as a five-year-old. He got plenty of experience and gained in strength last season. He travelled great in the Grade 1 at Aintree on his final start and looked like the winner going to the last, but he probably just didn't quite get the trip. I think he's going to keep on improving. A race like the Haldon Gold Cup at Exeter would suit him nicely and we'll make a plan after that."

Hurdler: Monmiral (h151p): "He was unbeaten last season and I think we're going to stay over hurdles. He could start off in the Fighting Fifth at Newcastle and then we'll see where we are. It's a tough year for these four-year-olds, but I'd rather go novice chasing with him as a five-year-old next season rather than as a four-year-old now."

Novice: Paso Doble (h124p): "He's a horse I really like. We gelded him when we bought him and gave him a bit of time. I didn't want to run him in just an ordinary maiden, so we put him in the Adonis at Kempton. He showed his lack of experience but ran really well and then won a maiden back at Kempton in the first week of May. He's done very well for his holiday and he's a proper horse, really exciting. He's one of a number of possibilities for the Persian War at Chepstow and there's a listed novice at Kempton after that to look at."

Fergal O'Brien

Wins-Runs in Britain in 2020/21	**104/563**
Highest-rated horse in training	**Silver Hallmark** Timeform Rating c147p

Chaser: Imperial Alcazar (h142): "We were going to go chasing with him last season. He ran very well when winning the Pertemps Qualifier at Warwick and then went for the Final at Cheltenham. He picked up an injury there but thankfully it wasn't too bad. He's back in full training and hopefully he'll make up into a lovely 3m novice chaser."

Hurdler: Alaphilippe (h134): "We'll start him off over hurdles and he might stick to that job depending on how he goes. He did very well for us last season, winning four from six. He won a Grade 2 at Haydock and ran well when finishing fifth in the Albert Bartlett at Cheltenham. He's a lovely, straightforward horse who goes very well on soft ground, but that's not a necessity for him. We're lucky to have him and he has options at Wetherby and Haydock to start off."

Novice: Peking Rose (b116): "He won first time out for us at Carlisle and then did very well at Ascot, finishing fourth in a listed race. He picked up a little niggle when we were schooling him to go over hurdles and his owners were very patient as we decided to wait and go to Aintree for the Grade 2 bumper. He ran an absolute blinder there to split the two Paul Nicholls-trained horses who beat him at Ascot and we're really looking forward to him going jumping."

Jonjo O'Neill

Wins-Runs in Britain in 2020/21	**71/479**
Highest-rated horse in training	**Cloth Cap** Timeform Rating c159

Chaser: Garry Clermont (c131p): "He got his act together at Warwick in soft ground over hurdles and that opens up a few more options for him. He will most likely go back chasing this season."

Hurdler: Soaring Glory (h142): "He was brilliant for us last year, winning the Betfair Hurdle, and he could either go chasing or stay hurdling this season. Hopefully he can keep progressing whichever route he takes."

Novice: Shantou's Melody (b95): "He's well related and a smart horse who won his bumper nicely. He's an exciting prospect to go novice hurdling with."

David Pipe

Wins-Runs in Britain in 2020/21	**52/346**
Highest-rated horse in training	**Ramses de Teillee** Timeform Rating c150

Chaser: Siruh du Lac (c150): "We were looking forward to running him in the Paddy Power Gold Cup at Cheltenham's November meeting, but he overjumped and unseated at the first. He pleased me in a schooling session thereafter but returned lame and that ruled him out for the remainder of the season. He has done well over the summer and remains a very exciting prospect for all the top handicap chases. We will probably try him over 3m at some point."

Hurdler: Gericault Roque (h123): "He did well last season, progressing nicely from finishing second in a Newton Abbot bumper to winning two of his three starts over timber. He showed a great attitude to score at Plumpton over the minimum trip before finding the sharp turns of Fakenham against him next time. His performance in winning at Sandown from an opening mark of 117 was very good and, with only five runs under his belt, this chasing type could improve further."

Novice: Colony Queen (f97): "She has joined us over the summer on the back of a fruitful campaign on the Flat which saw her win her last three starts. A lovely mare with a tremendous attitude, she has schooled well at home and looks an exciting type for novice hurdles for the season ahead."

Dan Skelton

Wins-Runs in Britain in 2020/21	**148/757**
Highest-rated horse in training	**Nube Negra** Timeform Rating c165+

Chaser: Nube Negra (c165+): "He will follow a very similar route to last season. With better ground he can be a top-class contender as he showed when second in the Champion Chase."

Hurdler: Calico (h140): "He was a good novice hurdler last season and has strengthened over the summer. He was a pretty high-class Flat horse and will obviously start in handicaps, but we hope he can be a great prospect in the bigger races."

Novice: My Drogo (h156p): "He was unbeaten in novice hurdles and we're looking forward to going chasing with him."

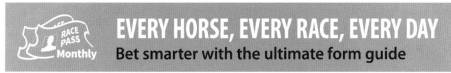

TALKING TO THE TRAINERS

Joe Tizzard

Wins-Runs in Britain in 2020/21	**37/433**
Highest-rated horse in training	**Native River** Timeform Rating c163

Chaser: Fiddlerontheroof (c147): "He progressed really well last season as a novice. He finished second a few times, but I think he was just coming up against real good horses, like Monkfish at the Cheltenham Festival. I think he's on a sensible mark and I can't wait to see him step up again this year. He'll probably head up to the Colin Parker at Carlisle for his first run and then maybe he'll have a crack at the Ladbrokes Trophy."

Hurdler: Oscar Elite (h136): "There's a chance we might leave him over hurdles. He was second in the Albert Bartlett at Cheltenham last season and we might have a campaign aiming towards the Stayers' Hurdle. He'll almost certainly start off in the West Yorkshire Hurdle at Wetherby and we'll just see where we are with him. If he was really competitive in that, then we could stay over hurdles with the Stayers' as a long-term target."

Novice: Sherborne (b84): "He finished second in a bumper at Hereford last season. He was still weak, but he's summered really well. He'll go novice hurdling in October, as soon as the ground is right, and I think he's a classy sort of horse."

Christian Williams

Wins-Runs in Britain in 2020/21	**16/211**
Highest-rated horse in training	**Kitty's Light** Timeform Rating c142

Chaser: Kitty's Light (c142): "He was a revelation last season and just kept improving. He's got a big engine and there doesn't seem to be a bottom to him, he always finishes his races really strongly. He's obviously got loads of ability and a good constitution. You could run him the next day or in the next race if it was possible, he comes out of his races very well. He's not an overly big horse but, if his jumping can keep improving like it did last season, who knows how far he can go? We'll probably go down the cross-country route with him, there's three nice races at Cheltenham to target him at. He'll enjoy those races and it will hopefully sharpen up his jumping. The big mid-season aim will be the Welsh National and then maybe the Scottish National. We see him as a Grand National horse of the future, but he's not qualified for Aintree next year because of his age."

Hurdler: Midnight Soldier (b85+): "He's a nice horse by Soldier of Fortune who won a bumper at Fontwell during the summer. He has schooled well all year and will probably start off at the first Cheltenham meeting in a maiden hurdle."

Novice: String To Your Bow (unraced under Rules): "He's a big horse by Getaway who ran in a point in Ireland for Donnchadh Doyle, who recommended him to us. He ran on quite a tight track and didn't get much luck in running, he got caught out quite wide and finished third. He's been showing us nice signs at home, so we look forward to going through the season with him. I would have thought he'll go straight down the novice hurdling route. We wouldn't be a big fan of running in bumpers and horses who start their education in points are already well schooled."

Evan Williams

Wins-Runs in Britain in 2020/21	**44/412**
Highest-rated horse in training	**Silver Streak** Timeform Rating h154

Chaser: Coconut Splash (c139p): "He hasn't won over fences but had a couple of runs last season and was probably badly placed by the trainer when you look at what beat him. He had a couple of tough assignments and his jumping needed to sharpen up. He might be better for having had the experience last season and he's a nice type of horse."

Hurdler: Champagne Rhythm (h119): "He's a devil of a horse to catch right in his races because, if you get there too soon, he thinks he's done enough. He can be a bit on and off the bridle and just a tricky old customer, but handicaps might suit him a damn sight better than novice hurdles. He's a difficult ride and needs producing literally right on the line."

Novice: Star Gate (h136): "He did nothing wrong over hurdles last season and fingers crossed fences will be a big help to him. He was still only a four-year-old when he finished second in the Challow at Newbury and he just needed a bit of time. He wants heavy ground to be seen at his best and he won't be seen until the real height of the winter. For a four-year-old last season, he did have a smashing novice hurdle campaign."

RISING STARS

Oliver Greenall

Base	**Stockton Hall Farm, Cheshire**
First Full Licence	**2016**
First Jumps Winner	**Jaunty Thor** Uttoxeter 12/11/2016
Total Winners	**97**
Best Horse Trained	**Pym** Timeform Rating c137

Oliver Greenall was Britain's men's champion point-to-point rider in the 2007/08 season with a record-breaking total of winners, following in the footsteps of his father Peter who won the same title four times in the 1980s, and who later, as Lord Daresbury, became chairman of Aintree racecourse. Greenall was also crowned champion amateur the following season, a title previously won twice by his brother Tom who himself also became champion between the flags. Having previously worked for Mick Easterby and trained pointers for six seasons, Greenall took out a full licence in 2016 after retiring from the saddle the year before. Barring the Covid-hit 2019/20 campaign, the stable's number of winners has increased each season, dramatically so in 2020/21 when reaching a total of 37 victories. That put Greenall in the top 20 trainers by number of winners and in the top 30 by total prize money which just topped £300,000. The yard's best-ever season ended on a high with its biggest win coming on the very last day at Sandown when juvenile hurdler Herbiers won his third race since joining Greenall from France, the Novices' Championship Final Handicap Hurdle worth £38,500 to the winner. Other winners of note were the useful front-running novice chaser Evander, who ended his campaign with a win at Ludlow, and useful staying chaser Late Romantic, who won a veterans' event at Haydock in December. An interesting acquisition from Nicky Henderson prior to the start of the current season was Pym, who showed smart form over fences for his former stable last autumn and showed he retains plenty of ability when second over hurdles at Uttoxeter in July. With a dozen winners on the board by the end of August, last season's total could well be under threat in the coming months.

Laura Morgan

Base	**Waltham On The Wolds, Leicestershire**
First Full Licence	**2016**
First Jumps Winner	**Flemi Two Toes** Southwell 11/12/2016
Total Winners	**67**
Best Horse Trained	**J'Ai Froid** Timeform Rating h146

Now training on the same gallops used by her father Kevin to whom she started out as assistant trainer, Laura Morgan gained valuable experience much further from home before taking out her own licence. That included a six-month spell in Australia with Peter Moody when outstanding sprinter Black Caviar was compiling her unbeaten record, followed by four years at Jackdaws Castle as Travelling Head Girl to Jonjo O'Neill. After training her first winner late in 2016, Laura Morgan notched 10 winners in 2017/18, most of those ridden by conditional Patrick Cowley, including four victories from novice chaser Skipping On. That horse contributed to the stable's eight wins the following season and, with winners at starting prices that included 66/1, 33/1, 22/1, 20/1 and 16/1, backing all the stable's runners blind that season would have returned a profit of £87.40 to a £1 stake! Last season Morgan's runners also returned a level-stakes profit, with a total of 25 winners more than double the stable's previous best tally and achieved at a strike rate of 22%. In a three-day spell in February, Morgan saddled four winners, including a double at Fakenham and a win at Ascot from staying hurdler J'Ai Froid, who was completing a hat-trick in his first season with the yard. J'Ai Froid made it four on the bounce at Warwick, all under conditional Max Kendrick, and, from a mark 37 lb higher than when starting his winning sequence in January, ended his season with an excellent second in a Grade 3 handicap at Aintree. Other good adverts for their trainer's skills were the novice chasers Fire Away and Overworkdunderpaid; the former ran up a hat-trick on his first three starts for the yard, while the latter won three of his first four starts on joining Morgan in the winter. Fire Away already has wins on the board this season, showing useful form when winning a handicap chase at Cartmel in May and then following up in a novice hurdle at Worcester in July.

Danny McMenamin

Attached Stable	**Nicky Richards**
First Ride	**2018**
First Winner	**Western Rules** Ayr 09/03/2018
Total Winners	**99**
Best Jumps Horses Ridden	**Nuts Well** Timeform Rating c158

Northern Ireland has already provided a couple of champion conditional jockeys who graduated to becoming champions in the senior ranks as well, so Danny McMenamin, born in County Down, will be hoping to follow in the footsteps of Sir Anthony McCoy and Brian Hughes. It was thanks to another well-known rider from the same part of the world, Tony Dobbin, that McMenamin made the move to Nicky Richards at Greystoke in 2017 where Dobbin had himself been stable jockey. Another former Greystoke jockey to play an important part in McMenamin's career to date is his coach Brian Harding. McMenamin's career under Rules got off to a perfect start when his very first ride was a winning one aboard Western Rules for Richards in an amateur riders' handicap hurdle at Ayr in March 2018. Still aged only 18 and with just five winners under his belt, McMenamin came to wider attention later the same year when landing the competitive Greatwood Handicap Hurdle at Cheltenham on Nietzsche for Brian Ellison, a win which McMenamin says "opened up a lot of doors for me after that and greatly aided my career". Seasonal totals of 16, 28 and 46 are proof of how McMenamin's career is progressing and last February he rode out his claim when landing his 75th career success on board Archie Brown at Market Rasen. Only seven of McMenamin's winners in 2020/21 were for his own stable, including an early-season hat-trick on hurdler Millie of Mayo, but the fact that his other winners came for 18 different trainers, most of them based in the North, shows that his services are widely in demand. As McMenamin readily acknowledges, that's due in no small part to being on the books of the north's leading jockey's agent Richard Hale alongside Brian Hughes. One trainer with whom McMenamin has struck up a particularly successful partnership is Ann Hamilton. When he won the Old Roan Chase at Aintree on Nuts Well it was his fifth success on that horse (the pair also finished second in the Melling Chase there later in the season), while McMenamin notched four wins during the latest season on stablemate Tommy's Oscar, whose campaign ended with a good third in the Scottish Champion Hurdle, and three on another useful novice Pay The Piper, who is a member of the *Fifty* for 2021/22.

Shane Fitzgerald

Attached Stable	**Joseph O'Brien/John Ryan**
First Ride	**2014**
First Winner	**Pull Again Green** Wexford 20/03/2021
Total Winners	**20**
Best Jumps Horses Ridden	**Assemble** Timeform Rating c148x

In their younger days in the saddle, Grand National-winning jockeys Davy Russell and Timmy Murphy were both champion novice riders two years running on the Irish point-to-point circuit. Aintree success is perhaps something to aspire to for the latest rider to have won back-to-back novice titles in 2017 and 2018, Shane Fitzgerald, who is now beginning to make a name for himself in the professional ranks. Fitzgerald has ridden more than 50 winners in Irish points, though as an amateur he had relatively few opportunities under Rules in the early years of his career since his first ride in 2014 and didn't get off the mark until March of the latest season when Pull Again Green won a bumper at Wexford. However, he has already had a ride at the Cheltenham Festival, partnering Clondaw Cian in the 2018 National Hunt Chase for Sussex trainer Suzy Smith. The same horse had provided Fitzgerald with his first winner in Irish points three years earlier. Fitzgerald made a dream start to life as a professional jockey when his very first ride as a pro, Fort William, was a 25/1 winner of a novice hurdle at Clonmel in May, albeit with a good slice of fortune. That was for Tipperary trainer John Ryan, who has been the main provider of Fitzgerald's winners so far with six victories. Fitzgerald has also ridden three winners for Joseph O'Brien, whose yard could well provide him with his best opportunities in the core part of the season. One of those winners for O'Brien formed part of Fitzgerald's career highlight to date which came at Tipperary in July where he rode a 1436/1 treble, including winners in the silks of both Gigginstown and J. P. McManus. O'Brien also provided Fitzgerald with a Galway Festival winner for Gigginstown, Desir du Large, while Fitzgerald conjured a better round of jumping than usual out of the same connections' error-prone chaser Assemble to finish a creditable seventh in the Galway Plate.

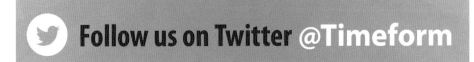

ANTE-POST BETTING

Timeform's John Ingles takes a look at the markets for some of the highlights in the National Hunt calendar and picks out his best value bets...

Last year's ante-post preview highlighted a couple of races from the Cheltenham Festival as being strong pieces of form to follow in the season ahead. The Supreme duly delivered, with the Nicky Henderson pair Shishkin and Chantry House, both successful at the Festival this time, enjoying highly successful novice chasing campaigns for the *Fifty*. The Albert Bartlett also lived up to expectations as a good source of winners, with ante-post pick Monkfish, selected here at 10/1, ultimately landing odds of 4/1-on in the 'RSA' or Brown Advisory Novices' Chase as it became. Now with two Festival wins on his CV, he's one we'll be keeping onside for Cheltenham next year, too. On the other hand, the Albert Bartlett also provided our Stayers' Hurdle fancy Thyme Hill who was also looking good until…more on that below, but hopefully we will get another bite or two, as well as the inevitable 'one that got away', as we go fishing again!

King George VI Chase

Wayward Lad, Desert Orchid and Kauto Star all had tremendous records at Kempton on Boxing Day, but each of them also had to bounce back from a defeat in the King George amongst multiple wins in the race. That's some comfort for the 2018 and 2019 winner **Clan des Obeaux**, who will be bidding to win back the title he lost to stablemate **Frodon** last season after being involved in a gruelling race at Haydock on his reappearance which seemed to leave its mark. It was a revitalised Clan des Obeaux that returned in cheekpieces in the spring to win at Aintree and Punchestown, and while the first of those races fell apart, his beating of former dual Gold Cup winner Al Boum Photo in the Punchestown Gold Cup was much more solid form. Having shown that the Gold Cup simply isn't his race, all the focus will surely be on Clan des Obeaux winning a third King George and Paul Nicholls will be keen to ensure he avoids a hard race beforehand this time. Much will depend on whether an Irish challenge materialises. Gold Cup runner-up **A Plus Tard** may be tempted to stay at home for the Savills Chase which he won last year, Cheveley Park Stud's other top-class chaser **Allaho** put up his best efforts over shorter trips last season, while the same owners' **Envoi Allen** began his novice season brilliantly but ended it with a fall at Cheltenham

Clan des Obeaux proves a class apart from his rivals at Aintree

and injury at Punchestown. **Chantry House**, on the other hand, completed his novice campaign with a Grade 1 double at Cheltenham and Aintree, but things very much went his way both times, and he'd need to take a big step forward if he's to provide Nicky Henderson with another King George winner.

SELECTIONS: Clan des Obeaux (5/1)

Champion Hurdle

Henry de Bromhead has confirmed that unbeaten reigning champion **Honeysuckle** will be remaining over hurdles with the aim of winning a second Champion Hurdle in March. She was a decisive winner at Cheltenham last season from the previous year's runner-up **Sharjah** and 2020 winner **Epatante**, and then took her unbeaten record to 12 when beating the same pair again with another dominant display at Punchestown. There's no reason to expect the outcome to be different in any future meetings between Honeysuckle and her established rivals, but what about some new challengers? Stablemate **Bob Olinger**, impressive winner of the Ballymore Novices'

Hurdle, looks set to go chasing instead, while Willie Mullins always had a similar future planned for **Appreciate It**, though his runaway win in the Supreme to remain unbeaten over hurdles gave his trainer something to think about. **Ferny Hollow** owes his place in the Champion Hurdle betting to wins over both the last-named pair but missed the rest of last season after defeating Bob Olinger on their respective hurdling debuts at Gowran. There are Champion Hurdle winners in Ferny Hollow's pedigree (Granville Again and Morley Street), but the 2020 Champion Bumper winner lacks hurdling experience and is another Mullins could send over fences. The same stable's **Echoes In Rain** was very impressive when winning a Grade 2 novice at Fairyhouse—less so when following up in a substandard Champion Novices' Hurdle at Punchestown— though the Mares' Hurdle may well be her target. In an Irish-dominated picture, there's scope for Paul Nicholls' unbeaten four-year-old **Monmiral** to stake his claim in the much less competitive environment of Britain's top 2m hurdles. He makes a bit more appeal among last season's juveniles than Triumph winner **Quilixios**, who ran poorly at Punchestown in a race that went to **Jeff Kidder**.

SELECTIONS: Monmiral (25/1 each-way)

Monmiral was Timeform's highest-rated juvenile hurdler in 2020/21

Queen Mother Champion Chase

One of the disappointments of last season's Cheltenham Festival was that the clash between unbeaten novice chasers **Shishkin** and **Energumene** never came off after the latter was forced to miss the Arkle with a setback. That left Shishkin to coast home for an impressive if bloodless win at Cheltenham before completing a simple task in more workmanlike fashion in the Maghull Novices' Chase at Aintree. Energumene was over his setback in time for Punchestown, however, and added to his Irish Arkle victory with another dominant performance in the Ryanair Novice Chase. All being well, Shishkin and Energumene will finally lock horns in the Queen Mother Champion Chase next March. While the ante-post betting heavily favours Shishkin to become Nicky Henderson's latest 2m chase champion, Timeform ratings have the pair separated by only a couple of pounds, so Energumene looks the value option at this stage. Given how many talented 2m chasers Willie Mullins has trained, it seems remarkable that he is still to win the Queen Mother Champion Chase. **Chacun Pour Soi** fluffed his lines when odds on for the latest edition, finishing only third, but if he's able to repeat the sort of performance which then saw him beat stablemate and impressive Ryanair Chase winner **Allaho** in the Champion Chase at Punchestown, he'll be very much the one his two younger rivals have to beat. It all points to the first two from last season's Queen Mother Champion Chase, **Put The Kettle On** and **Nube Negra**, facing a stiffer task in the next edition. Nube Negra was a long way behind Chacun Pour Soi when third at Punchestown, while Put The Kettle On was beaten in Britain for the first time when **Greaneteen**, only fourth at Cheltenham, took the scalp of former champion **Altior** in the Celebration Chase at Sandown.

SELECTIONS: Energumene (5/1)

Stayers' Hurdle

Readers who took the 16/1 recommended here for **Thyme Hill** in last season's Stayers' Hurdle doubtless found themselves agreeing with trainer Philip Hobbs that it was "very bad timing" when a pulled muscle ruled him out of the race less than a week beforehand, by which time he was vying for favouritism. There was compensation, at least for Thyme Hill, when he won the Liverpool Hurdle at Aintree three weeks later, and as a result he's disputing favouritism in an open market for the 2022 Stayers' Hurdle. In truth, he might have struggled to peg back Gavin Cromwell's much-improved six-year-old **Flooring Porter**, who put up a high-class effort when making all at Cheltenham to beat **Sire du Berlais** and former winner **Paisley Park**, who'd been involved in some close tussles with Thyme Hill earlier in the season. That was just about the best performance in this division and it looks a bit of an overreaction by some layers to push Flooring Porter out to double-figure odds following a run that was

Galopin des Champs wins the Martin Pipe at the Cheltenham Festival

too bad to be true at Punchestown. The Champion Stayers Hurdle at Punchestown was won in good style by former Supreme winner **Klassical Dream** for Willie Mullins, having his first start for well over a year and trying 3m for the first time. Making more appeal for the Stayers' Hurdle, though, is another Mullins winner at Punchestown, **Galopin des Champs**, who became the stable's latest winner of the Martin Pipe at Cheltenham before proving himself much better than a handicapper when following up by 12 lengths in the Grade 1 novice over 3m. As a lightly-raced five-year-old, there's no hurry to go chasing with him just yet and he won't have too much more improvement to make to challenge the leading stayers.

SELECTIONS: Galopin des Champs (10/1)

Cheltenham Gold Cup

The Cheltenham Gold Cup is another race where Irish-trained horses dominate the ante-post betting. Six of the last eight Gold Cups have gone to Ireland, with the Henry de Bromhead pair **Minella Indo** and **A Plus Tard** taking the first two places last year ahead of **Al Boum Photo**, who was favourite to win the race for the third year running for Willie Mullins. Al Boum Photo ran to a similar level in defeat as he had done for his two Gold Cup wins and did so again when runner-up to Clan des Obeaux at Punchestown.

Al Boum Photo simply ran into two better, and younger, rivals at Cheltenham and that age difference could be an important factor as no horse as old as 10 has won the Gold Cup this century. The De Bromhead pair, on the other hand, neither of whom was seen out after Cheltenham, have relative youth on their side and are fully entitled to be leading contenders again in 2022. There's much less between them, though, than the betting suggests. A Plus Tard, a year younger than Minella Indo and unexposed over 3m+, shouldn't be twice the price of his stablemate which he is in some places. Their stable-companion **Envoi Allen** looked hugely exciting in novice chases for much of the season but needs to prove himself again after failing to complete his last two starts, pulled up lame in the Champion Novice Chase at Punchestown. The same race saw the first defeat over fences for another of Ireland's top novices **Monkfish** (beaten by stablemate Colreevy on her final start before going to stud), but he looks well worth another chance to build on an impressive win at Leopardstown in February and has been a Cheltenham Festival winner for each of the last two years.

SELECTIONS: Monkfish (6/1)

Grand National

As an Aintree first-timer, Grand National winner **Minella Times** offered further proof that nowadays prior experience over the course isn't key to finding the winner. Indeed, he wouldn't have shown up on any long-range radar for the race, either, having begun the season needing to make at least a stone's worth of improvement just to secure a place in the line-up. He'd also won only one of his seven starts over fences the previous season and had run only once over as far as 3m. It's a very different story now, as Minella Times is vying for favouritism for the 2022 Grand National with another J. P. McManus contender, **Any Second Now**, who finished third but might have been the winner himself with a better run. **Galvin**, who completed an unbeaten season in the National Hunt Chase, and the novices who finished second and fourth in the Irish Grand National, **Run Wild Fred** and **Latest Exhibition**, are other leading Irish contenders for Aintree at this stage. But some young British-trained chasers emerged in the spring as future Grand National types, notably the Midlands Grand National winner **Time To Get Up** and the Scottish Grand National winner **Mighty Thunder**, who had finished runner-up at Uttoxeter. Trained by Jonjo O'Neill and Lucinda Russell respectively, they have the additional recommendation of coming from yards that know how to prepare a Grand National winner. Kim Bailey has trained the winner before, too, and his **Happygolucky**, winner of the Grade 3 handicap on the Grand National card, could be back for the big one with another year's experience. Irish-trained chasers accounted for 10 of the first 11 finishers in last season's Grand National, but they'll do well to be quite so dominant in 2022 and we'll pick one from each side of the Irish Sea for our selections.

SELECTIONS: Time To Get Up (25/1), Latest Exhibition (33/1)

JUMPABILITY RATINGS

Timeform Analyst Graeme North explains the concept of 'jumpability' and reveals which novice chasers performed best by this measure during the latest season.

The new National Hunt season is just around the corner and with it comes the tantalising prospect of last season's top chasing prospects Shishkin and Energumene moving out of novice company. How will their jumping stand up against the best of the established chasers around do we think? Can we even measure how well they jump?

Well, yes, we can and have been doing internally at Timeform for some years. We call the metric 'jumpability'. For those readers unfamiliar with the concept, 'jumpability' is an attempt to assign a 'jumping' rating to a chaser that measures jumping ability, much as a form rating reflects merit, and is calculated by utilising data that exists within the Timeform database.

For many years now, Timeform has recorded for every performance (where one is deserved) 'in-play symbols'—effectively a short-hand notation that indicates noteworthy positive or negative aspects of a horse's performance, two of which are x (or X) and j (or J). Long-time readers will be familiar with the x as it sometimes appears alongside a rating (or by itself) in the Timeform racecard, denoting a poor jumper (or, if xx, a very bad jumper). Contrastingly, a j (which isn't a racecard symbol) signifies that the horse jumped well or, if awarded a J, outstandingly well.

From that starting point, 'jumpability' ratings are then prompted by allotting a 0 or 'jump neutral' value to the horse if they have neither an x nor j in-play symbol for a particular race and didn't fall or unseat; a negative value if they attracted an x or an X and a positive value for either j or J. Falls and unseats are negated by a j or J, while Xs and falls/unseats are not counted twice within the same race. Those values are then set against all the tracks at which the horse has run, as some courses have easy fences (Lingfield, for example) while others have stiff fences (Cheltenham).

To complete the calculation, those figures are then tweaked further after accounting for field size, race distance, race type ('novice' or 'beginners' races as opposed to handicaps, for example) and underfoot conditions (because longer distance races in the mud are more likely to prompt jumping errors than small-field affairs over short distances on good ground). The resulting jumpability rating is recalculated after every run. Horses that have had less than eight races are treated as jump neutral for each 'missing' race so as not to wrongly label a horse either a superb or terrible jumper based on insufficient runs. And that's it!

Tables showing the easiest and hardest jumping tests in Britain and Ireland, as well as the leading jumpability ratings since 2010, and the leading jumpability ratings for any horse that was a novice in 2020/21, are shown below.

Easiest (GB)	Hardest (GB)	Easiest (Ire)	Hardest (Ire)
Lingfield Park	Aintree (combined)	Naas	Listowel
Uttoxeter	Fakenham	Roscommon	Thurles
Leicester	Cheltenham (combined)	Downpatrick	Leopardstown
Hexham	Newbury	Killarney	Fairyhouse
Carlisle	Taunton	Kilbeggan	Down Royal

LEADING JUMPABILITY SINCE 2010

Horse	Rating	Horse	Rating
Altior	91	Chacun Pour Soi	60
Sprinter Sacre	87	Rebel Fitz	58
Douvan	67	Vroum Vroum Mag	58
Many Clouds	66	Brandon Hill	57
Sir Note	66	Trifolium	57
Notebook	64	Presentandcounting	57
Sanctuaire	64	Captain Conan	56
Siruh Du Lac	63	Ainsi Fideles	55
Put The Kettle On	62	Cyrname	54
Funambule Sivola	61	Cloth Cap	53

LEADING 2020/21 NOVICES

Horse	Rating	Horse	Rating
Funambule Sivola	61	The Mulcair	41
Shan Blue	53	Shishkin	39
Editeur Du Gite	51	Absolute Jaffa	39
Fidelio Vallis	51	El Presente	38
Slanelough	51	Jersey Bean	37
Remastered	50	Marown	37
High Up In The Air	46	Kiruna Peak	37
Lieutenant Rocco	45	Five Star Getaway	36
Messire Des Obeaux	44	Ga Law	35
Darling Maltaix	43	Flagrant Delitiep	35

The first thing to notice is that not unexpectedly the best jumpers over the last 10 seasons include some very familiar names whose longevity at the top of their tree is in part due to their jumping prowess. One-time stable-companions Altior and Sprinter Sacre dominate the list (the ratings are set on a 100 to -100 scale with 100 being outstanding, 0 being neither good nor bad and -100 appalling), while the leading Irish-trained runner is the memorable Douvan.

So far as looking ahead to the 2021/22 season is concerned, it's interesting to note that one novice from last season makes the best-since-2010 top 20 list, Funambule Sivola. He was one of the most improved of his ilk last season, winning his first handicap off a BHA mark of 112 and his last off 143 after which he ran a career best against Shishkin in a good time at Aintree. Still only six, he has got scope for more improvement and certainly won't be held back by his jumping.

Shan Blue is another whose jumping will stand him in good stead, while Editeur du Gite is one who could land a good handicap given that his clean jumping and front-running style is sure to take many of his rivals out of their comfort zone.

So, what of last season's other leading novices? Well, Shishkin didn't quite make the top ten novices last season (twelfth) but, for all he has made the odd error in his races, he put in an exemplary round of jumping on his debut at Kempton and also earned a small j for his effort in the Arkle. His main rival in last year's novice division Energumene falls outside the top 20 with a jumpability score of 31, but that shouldn't put anyone off. He was awarded a J when winning the Irish Arkle at Leopardstown and showed he was over the issue that kept him away from Cheltenham with a near-flawless display in the Grade 1 Ryanair Novice Chase at the Punchestown Festival.

Energumene's jumping stood up well in three very strongly-run races last season, all races in which he earned timefigures well into the 160s, and, for me at least on that count, looks the most interesting novice venturing out into open company.

SECTION

TIMEFORM'S VIEW

Chosen from the Timeform Formbook, here is Timeform's detailed analysis—compiled by our team of race reporters and supplemented by observations from Timeform's handicappers—of a selection of key races from Cheltenham and Aintree.

CHELTENHAM Tuesday March 16
GOOD to SOFT

Sky Bet Supreme Novices' Hurdle (Grade 1) (1)

Pos	Btn	Horse	Age	Wgt	Eq	Trainer	Jockey	SP
1		APPRECIATE IT (IRE)	7	11-7		W. P. Mullins, Ireland	P. Townend	8/11f
2	24	BALLYADAM (IRE)	6	11-7		Henry de Bromhead, Ireland	J. W. Kennedy	6/1
3	2¼	FOR PLEASURE (IRE)	6	11-7		Alex Hales	Harry Bannister	40/1
4	1¼	SOARING GLORY (IRE)	6	11-7	(s)	Jonjo O'Neill	Jonjo O'Neill Jr.	10/1
5	5½	IRASCIBLE (FR)	6	11-7		Henry de Bromhead, Ireland	Rachael Blackmore	25/1
6	1½	GRUMPY CHARLEY	6	11-7		Chris Honour	Bryan Carver	28/1
7	1¼	METIER (IRE)	5	11-7		Harry Fry	Sean Bowen	11/2
F		BLUE LORD (FR)	6	11-7		W. P. Mullins, Ireland	Daryl Jacob	11/1

8 ran   Race Time 3m 57.00   Closing Sectional (3.90f): 57.6s (97.8%)   Winning Owner: Miss M. A. Masterson

A year on from a Cheltenham Festival that has become in some quarters the whipping boy for the whole British approach to the Covid-19 pandemic, began a Festival, one must hope, like no other, staged behind closed doors, a symbolic moment nonetheless for racing's ability to keep the show on the road almost without incident since June, at a time when many other shows have had closure notices up the whole time, credit due to the BHA and all of racing's other stakeholders that there is racing to report on; the show began with just 8 runners in the Supreme, a division of the Gloucestershire Hurdle, its predecessor, having had 9 in 1950, though it was quantity rather than quality that was missing, the absence of social/speculative runners not a great loss in truth, My Drogo the one obvious absentee, accepting the top juveniles would go for the Triumph, the winner producing a performance right up there with the best recent victors in the race, though his margin of victory would have been considerably less had Blue Lord, running a race full of promise, not fallen at the last; the race was well run and a very good test under conditions that weren't quite so soft as officially described. **Appreciate It** beaten only in the Champion Bumper since debut, made up for that reverse, when a warm favourite, producing a performance right out of the top drawer, one that entitles him to be spoken of in the same terms as the best recent winners of this race, Douvan and Altior; tracked pace, jumped well, travelled strongly, pressed leader 3 out, went on next, quickened clear straight, kept on well run-in, impressive; he's a real powerhouse to look at, outstanding in a good field, and every inch a chaser, and though he's bred to stay a good deal further than 2m, he seems likely to follow the same path as Altior and Shishkin and attempt to win the 2022 Arkle, already a short price to do so. **Ballyadam** moved from Gordon Elliott earlier in the month, was even further behind Appreciate It than he had been at Leopardstown, bungling 2 out having only a marginal impact; patiently ridden, took keen hold, smooth headway 3 out, close up when clouted 2 out, outpaced after, keeping on when left disputing second last; like the winner and Blue Lord he has chaser written all over him and he should make a smart performer in that division next season. **For Pleasure** must be a fantastic horse to own and ran his heart out again, his jumping keeping him in the game until the second last before his effort took its toll; led, jumped superbly, went with zest, clear until third, challenged 3 out, headed next, left behind by winner, left disputing second last, one paced; he would take some catching in the Swinton on good ground. **Soaring Glory** bizarrely, frankly, in first-time cheekpieces, wasn't in the same form as at Newbury, the headgear seeming to buzz him up in a race that was always on the cards to be well run anyway; held up, not settle fully, shaken up after 3 out, left behind soon after next; hopefully this will prove a blip, and he'll be a smart prospect for novice chasing next season. **Irascible** much more patiently ridden than when taking on Appreciate It at Leopardstown, lacked experience and probably wants more of a test of stamina than this provided, not comfortable with the pace a long way out; soon behind, off the bridle long way out, never on terms. **Grumpy Charley** found less testing ground away from Chepstow rather more than he could cope with, raised considerably in class; raced off the pace, labouring before third. **Metier** who had missed the Betfair Hurdle to wait for this, flopped, his stable rather struggling for winners since the turn of the year, his form in the Tolworth perhaps not quite so good as it might have appeared, in touch, travelled well, shaken up after 3 out, weakened soon after next. **Blue Lord** running here in preference to the County Hurdle, was running a fine race for one with so little experience when he took an unfortunate fall at the last, around 8 lengths down on the winner and, though likely to have been beaten further still, set to finish well clear of the rest; waited with, travelled smoothly, chased leader after 2 out, keeping on when fell last; he has further improvement over hurdles in him, but he looks more a chaser and should make a smart novice next season.

Sporting Life Arkle Challenge Trophy Novices' Chase (Grade 1) (1)

Pos	Btn	Horse	Age	Wgt	Eq	Trainer	Jockey	SP
1		SHISHKIN (IRE)	7	11-4		Nicky Henderson	Nico de Boinville	4/9f
2	12	ELDORADO ALLEN (FR)	7	11-4	(t)	Colin Tizzard	Harry Cobden	33/1
3	1	CAPTAIN GUINNESS (IRE)	6	11-4		Henry de Bromhead, Ireland	Rachael Blackmore	10/1
4	½	ALLMANKIND	5	11-4	(h+t)	Dan Skelton	Harry Skelton	5/1
5	26	FRANCO DE PORT (FR)	6	11-4		W. P. Mullins, Ireland	P. Townend	8/1

5 ran Race Time 3m 54.30 Closing Sectional (3.75f): 56.00s (98.7%) Winning Owner: Mrs J Donnelly

The theme over the past decade has been of dominant performers but a lack of depth overall in the 2m novice chase division, this year looking a bit different until Energumene was ruled out through lameness the Friday before, thereby robbing the race of a top-billing, Anglo-Irish clash between a pair of unbeaten chasers; that said, any resulting doubts about how strongly the race would be run were soon cast aside when Captain Guinness carted his way forward to join Allmankind from the third, those 2 ensuring the race was every bit the test of jumping at speed it's designed to be, only Shishkin of the other trio able to stay in touch and asked to take it up from the pair of trailblazers as far out as the third last before coasting away in the latter stages, the race very reminiscent of the 2018 renewal won by Footpad, including a runner-up who picked up the pieces very late. **Shishkin** had no Energumene to drive him on but still stamped himself as the leading novice chaser at 2m, with the prospect of even better to come over further in due course, not that connections will likely be in any rush to step him up with other powerhouses Envoi Allen and Monkfish in the same generation, easy to see him dominating the open 2m division in Britain next season; relaxed in the paddock and looking very well, he was the only one able to stay in touch with the pair of leaders, lost ground briefly with them when had to put himself right 5 out but right back on terms soon after the next and taking control of the race 3 out, sauntering clear in the straight; both Altior and Sprinter Sacre ran again the season they won the Arkle so hopefully we'll get to see Shishkin at Aintree or Sandown, and, while he's not at Sprinter Sacre's level yet, he's arguably got at least as much potential as that pair did at the same stage, with the prospect of Energumene pushing him to such heights should they meet next season. **Eldorado Allen** fitted with a tongue strap and on his toes beforehand, matched his previous form but was seemingly flattered in finishing second, certainly ridden for that position; held up, untidy first, again third, off pace still 3 out, stayed on to take second final 50 yds; he's reached a smart level around 2m and will surely be even better over further. **Captain Guinness** representing Energumene's form, didn't give his true running, just too keen to do himself justice, like the yard's Notebook in the race last year; late into the paddock and very much on his toes, he pulled his way to the front at the third and exchanged the lead with Allmankind until 3 out, jumping boldly, was slightly hampered soon after and lost second before the home turn, no match for the winner and able to find just the one pace in the straight. **Allmankind** has taken to chasing better than might have been expected (outclassed physically in this field) and is better than the bare form, having his chance compromised by the free-going Captain Guinness, shaping second best for all he ended up only fourth; led, joined third and exchanged the lead from there, not fluent fifth, untidy 3 out and briefly dropped back to third, untidy again last, lost second only final 50 yds; that said, it's quite hard to see him taking his form up any further in the open division next season. **Franco de Port** had already won a Grade 1 novice chase at around this trip but was simply run off his feet in a strongly-run race on drying ground, though it should be pointed out that he also flopped when fancied for the Coral Cup last year, perhaps an unhappy traveller; soon behind, uncomfortable with pace, slow fifth, again eighth, beaten long way out.

Unibet Champion Hurdle Challenge Trophy (Grade 1) (1)

Pos	Btn	Horse	Age	Wgt	Eq	Trainer	Jockey	SP
1		HONEYSUCKLE	7	11-3		Henry de Bromhead, Ireland	Rachael Blackmore	11/10f
2	6½	SHARJAH (FR)	8	11-10	(t)	W. P. Mullins, Ireland	P. Townend	11/1
3	3	EPATANTE (FR)	7	11-3		Nicky Henderson	Aidan Coleman	4/1
4	1½	ASPIRE TOWER (IRE)	5	11-10		Henry de Bromhead, Ireland	Robbie Power	33/1
5	2	NOT SO SLEEPY	9	11-10		Hughie Morrison	Jonathan Burke	125/1
6	1¼	SILVER STREAK (IRE)	8	11-10		Evan Williams	Tom O'Brien	22/1
7	¾	SALDIER (FR)	7	11-10		W. P. Mullins, Ireland	D. E. Mullins	80/1
8	11	GOSHEN (FR)	5	11-10		Gary Moore	Jamie Moore	11/2
9	6	JAMES DU BERLAIS (FR)	5	11-10		W. P. Mullins, Ireland	Daryl Jacob	14/1
F		ABACADABRAS (FR)	7	11-10	(t)	Mrs Denise Foster, Ireland	J. W. Kennedy	10/1

10 ran Race Time 3m 55.50 Closing Sectional (3.90f): 55.5s (100.9%) Winning Owner: Mr K. Alexander

A vintage winning performance in the blue riband of hurdling, even if the cupboard in the division continues to be pretty bare, Honeysuckle's route to victory eased by her main market rivals not being at their best, though they would have struggled to land a blow even if they had been, her performance above average for the race since the days of Hurricane Fly at least, fair to say that the sex allowance enhanced her margin of victory rather than made a difference to the outcome, though a third successful mare in the race in the last 6 runnings may raise the question of that allowance—brought in just in time for Dawn

Run—though removing it would surely have the effect of driving the top mares towards the David Nicholson, which is not for the overall good, surely; the race was run at a sound pace and the form looks very straightforward to interpret. **Honeysuckle** maintained her unbeaten record in taking the biggest hurdling prize of all, scoring in most decisive fashion and running to a level that would have made her hard to beat (with the sex allowance) in the majority of recent runnings of the race, those that supported her down to such a short price scarcely having a moment's worry, sound jumping and a good turn of foot, hallmarks of so many winners of this race, very much in evidence; in touch, took keen hold, smooth headway before 3 out, quickened to lead soon after 2 out, in command before last, kept on well, impressive; she's now won 11 from 11 and has yet to look in serious trouble in a race, to say that she'll continue to be very hard to beat no more than stating the obvious. **Sharjah** was quickly back to form, at least as good as ever in taking second for the second year running, well served by the way the race was run; held up, travelled well, headway after 3 out, chased leader approaching last, stayed on, no match for winner. **Epatante** had been treated for a back problem since her defeat at Kempton, but there wasn't the same confidence behind her in the market as there had been a year earlier and she wasn't in the same form that had seen her win so well then, though even if she had been she would have been up against it with the winner; patiently ridden, effort approaching 2 out, not quicken home turn, plugged on run-in; connections may be tempted by a rematch with the winner at Punchestown, though a try over further at Aintree would be an alternative. **Aspire Tower** ran well at the meeting for a second time, having his chance and needing no excuses; handy, went second fourth, led briefly 2 out, jumped left there, left behind by winner entering straight, one paced last. **Not So Sleepy** ran about as well as could have been expected back up in grade, not asked to lead for once; prominent, not settle fully, ridden 3 out, lost place soon after, kept on again last; he's not going to be easy to place over hurdles, so perhaps the Chester Cup might be an option, back on the Flat. **Silver Streak** was below form, slightly surprising that tactics which suited the circumstances at Kempton were repeated in a race where they seemed less likely to pay off, the early effort telling against him in the latter stages; led, shaken up 3 out, headed when hampered next, no extra approaching last. **Saldier** took a step forward from a low base, though without looking remotely competitive; dropped out, hampered third, mistake fourth, pushed along after fifth, plugged on straight, never on terms. **Goshen** was a major disappointment, ironically the fears about his going left handed that failed to materialise when they were the main talking point before last season's Triumph, turning up unwelcome after they'd been forgotten about this time around; prominent, hung badly right from third, weakened after 3 out; he's going to have limited options at 2m if he needs to go right handed over hurdles—Punchestown this spring—and it may be that novice chasing is an option next season. **James du Berlais** a smart 4-y-o hurdler for Robert Collet last year, runner-up in a Group 1 at Auteuil in November, hadn't been able to have a prep run for his new yard and finished well held, thrown in at the deep end; in touch, ridden 3 out, lost place soon after; it's early days with him, so far as his new trainer is concerned. **Abacadabras** who'd given Shishkin a race in the Supreme last season, seemed likely to be suited by the run of the race, but didn't get the chance to show what he could do; held up, fell third.

TIMEFORM'S VIEW

CHELTENHAM Wednesday March 17
GOOD to SOFT

Ballymore Novices' Hurdle (Baring Bingham) (Grade 1) (1)

Pos	Btn	Horse	Age	Wgt	Eq	Trainer	Jockey	SP
1		BOB OLINGER (IRE)	6	11-7		Henry de Bromhead, Ireland	Rachael Blackmore	6/4f
2	7½	GAILLARD DU MESNIL (FR)	5	11-7	(h)	W. P. Mullins, Ireland	P. Townend	9/4
3	4½	BRAVEMANSGAME (FR)	6	11-7		Paul Nicholls	Harry Cobden	4/1
4	½	BEAR GHYLLS (IRE)	6	11-7		Nicky Martin	Matt Griffiths	15/2
5	7½	DOES HE KNOW	6	11-7	(h)	Kim Bailey	David Bass	50/1
6	1½	KESKONRISK (FR)	6	11-7	(t)	Joseph Patrick O'Brien, Ireland	Donagh Meyler	20/1
7	44	OPTIMISE PRIME (IRE)	5	11-7		Ben Pauling	Daryl Jacob	80/1

7 ran Race Time 5m 06.50 Closing Sectional (3.90f): 55.8s (102.0%) Winning Owner: Robcour

As with the Supreme the day before, this was the smallest field assembled for the Baring Bingham in its current form, but similarly it was very much a case of quality over quantity, with 3 last-time-out winners of Grade 1 novices in opposition, and it produced a winner of almost limitless potential, Bob Olinger, just the most gorgeous chasing type to look at, who ran to a level at least on a par with such recent victors as Envoi Allen, Samcro, Faugheen and The New One, behind only Simonsig among winners in the last decade, every chance that he will reach some of the heights that quintet have done; the race was soundly run and there were no obvious excuses for the beaten horses, though Bear Ghylls would have finished closer with even a halfway fluent round of jumping. **Bob Olinger** faced stiffer opposition than previously (though Blue Lord, runner-up at Naas last time, would have run well in the Supreme but for falling) and passed the test with flying colours, running to a level right up there with previous good winners of this race and marking himself clearly one of the very best prospects around; held up, pulled way into prominent position before fourth, not fluent seventh, led on bridle 2 out, quickened clear early in straight, impressive; he's been beaten only by the Champion Bumper winner Ferny Hollow (unfortunately on the sidelines since) in 4 starts over hurdles and, being a rangy, good sort on looks, has top-class chaser written all over him, a really thrilling prospect for the switch to fences next autumn. **Gaillard du Mesnil** back down in trip, didn't have the pace of the winner from the turn but stuck to his task and ran at least as well as last time; waited with, not settle fully, loomed up approaching 2 out, not quicken after, mistake last, stayed on; he's less obviously a chaser on looks than the other principals, though that may well be where he heads next season, likely to continue to give a good account whatever route is chosen. **Bravemansgame** facing his toughest test yet, was essentially outclassed and outspeeded, his record over hurdles still a really positive one, given he looks much more a chasing type; pressed leader, went on before third, headed when not fluent 2 out, left behind by winner before last, no extra run-in. **Bear Ghylls** lost his unbeaten record, but he ran well up considerably in class and might well have done even better had he jumped more fluently, making errors at at least half the flights; raced wide, in touch, jumped none too fluently, not settle fully, chased leader seventh, every chance when mistake next, blundered 2 out, outpaced home turn, kept on well run-in; on looks and demeanour, he is every inch a chaser and should do well at that discipline next season. **Does He Know** had a lot on in this company and wasn't up to the task, but he ended up running creditably, probably helped by the return to less testing ground; held up, not fluent second, mistake sixth, left behind 3 out; he has the physique to make a chaser next season. **Keskonrisk** upped markedly in trip, didn't appear to stay, though it was asking a lot of him to tackle this company on such a small amount of experience; held up, not fluent seventh, shaken up after, not fluent next, mistake 2 out, weakened straight. **Optimise Prime** was out of his depth; led until before third, lost place after fourth, ridden when mistake seventh, left behind next.

Brown Advisory Novices' Chase (Broadway) (Grade 1) (1)

Pos	Btn	Horse	Age	Wgt	Eq	Trainer	Jockey	SP
1		MONKFISH (IRE)	7	11-4		W. P. Mullins, Ireland	P. Townend	1/4f
2	6½	FIDDLERONTHEROOF (IRE)	7	11-4	(t)	Colin Tizzard	Robbie Power	40/1
3	11	THE BIG BREAKAWAY (IRE)	6	11-4		Colin Tizzard	Harry Cobden	12/1
4	41	DICKIE DIVER (IRE)	8	11-4		Nicky Henderson	Aidan Coleman	33/1
F		SPORTING JOHN (IRE)	6	11-4		Philip Hobbs	Richard Johnson	16/1
ur		EKLAT DE RIRE (FR)	7	11-4		Henry de Bromhead, Ireland	Rachael Blackmore	10/1

6 ran Race Time 6m 12.30 Closing Sectional (3.75f): 55.1s (104.0%) Winning Owner: Mrs S. Ricci

A new name and an old one for the staying novice chase championship, RSA having ended the last remaining original sponsorship among events in the Jumps Pattern, requiring a registered name to be added, the former name of the race, the Broadway, pressed into action; sadly, it was far from a vintage renewal, with the best of the British-trained staying novices aimed elsewhere, including Royale Pagaille, who is in the same ownership, and Monkfish was sent off at very short odds in a field that was clearly substandard overall, even more so when Eklat de Rire departed, the bare form of the win on a par with that shown by the principals in a strong renewal of the NH Chase the day before, any of the first 3 there likely to have made more of a race of it with the winner. **Monkfish** held outstanding form claims and didn't have to run near the level he managed at Leopardstown last time, gaining a second Festival win after landing the Spa a year earlier, a Gold Cup bid the obvious aim for a third, though his jumping would need to be a bit sharper than it was here; led, not fluent second, mistake eighth, headed, led again 3 out, kicked on straight, in control when mistake last, shaken up after, kept on; essentially he won with more authority than the bare margin implies and he remains capable of better. **Fiddlerontheroof** ran well in first-time tongue strap, ridden to take advantage of any flaws in the favourite after his own stable companion had tried to soften him up, though there proved to be none; held up, travelled well, mistake fourteenth, shaken up before 3 out, went second straight, stayed on, no impression on winner. **The Big Breakaway** wasn't disgraced, a bit better than the final distances imply, paying for trying to put it up to the winner for a long way; tracked pace, upsides third, fourth, led eighth, headed when mistake 3 out, no extra before last. **Dickie Diver** ran no sort of race, asking a lot of him to tackle this on just his second start over fences, his jumping totally unconvincing; not jump well, always behind. **Sporting John** ought to have been suited by the longer trip but the fences got in the way; held up, bad mistake eleventh, pushed along soon after and essentially unable to recover, behind when fell heavily 2 out. **Eklat de Rire** might well have given the winner more to think about, but he departed in unfortunate circumstances soon after halfway; in touch, travelled well, pecked and unseated rider twelfth.

Betway Queen Mother Champion Chase (Grade 1) (1)

Pos	Btn	Horse	Age	Wgt	Eq	Trainer	Jockey	SP
1		PUT THE KETTLE ON (IRE)	7	11-3		Henry de Bromhead, Ireland	Aidan Coleman	17/2
2	½	NUBE NEGRA (SPA)	7	11-10	(t)	Dan Skelton	Harry Skelton	11/1
3	1	CHACUN POUR SOI (FR)	9	11-10		W. P. Mullins, Ireland	P. Townend	8/13f

4	½	GREANETEEN (FR)	7	11-10		Paul Nicholls	Harry Cobden	50/1
5	1¾	SCEAU ROYAL (FR)	9	11-10		Alan King	Daryl Jacob	16/1
6	2¾	FIRST FLOW (IRE)	9	11-10		Kim Bailey	David Bass	11/1
7	2¾	NOTEBOOK (GER)	8	11-10	(t)	Henry de Bromhead, Ireland	Rachael Blackmore	22/1
8	11	CILAOS EMERY (FR)	9	11-10	(h)	W. P. Mullins, Ireland	B. J. Cooper	12/1
9	1½	ROUGE VIF (FR)	7	11-10	(t)	Harry Whittington	Gavin Sheehan	20/1

9 ran   Race Time 3m 57.80   Closing Sectional (3.75f): 54.60s (102.7%)   Winning Owner: One For Luck Racing Syndicate

A result that will further stoke the argument over the merits of the mares' allowance at the highest level, Put The Kettle On becoming the first of her sex to ever win this, following up her win in last year's Arkle, that particular double far from uncommon; the race overall has to go down as rather unsatisfactory, dual winner Altior again forced out of the race a couple of days beforehand, last year's winner Politologue a last-minute withdrawal after he was found to have blood in a nostril on saddling, the gallop not as quick as expected and the field still very well grouped when there was major trouble on the inside after the third last, Sceau Royal the worst affected, doing remarkably well to finish where he did after that, while connections of the runner-up could also count themselves a little unfortunate with him having had to switch around the winner on the run-in; perhaps the biggest deflation post-race, however, centred around the favourite Chacun Pour Soi who seemed to have been delivered perfectly but didn't have enough in reserve after racing keenly; incidentally, Henry de Bromhead has saddled the winners of the first 2 championship races of the week, a feat also achieved by Nicky Henderson in 2018 but not before that since Fred Winter sent out Bula and Crisp in 1971, while no trainer has added the Gold Cup to wins in the Champion Hurdle and Champion Chase in the same year, something de Bromhead has chances of doing on Friday. **Put The Kettle On** was leant a hand by Chacun Pour Soi's wobble, as well as trouble in behind, not to mention a mares' allowance, arguments over the validity of which at the top level promise to rumble on, but to focus on any one of those 3 factors would do a huge disservice to a mare who is as tough and hearty as they come, her tenacity showcased to the full back at a track at which she excels, following up her win in last year's Arkle to become the first ever mare to win the Champion Chase; very much on her toes and mounted outside the paddock, having led early she pressed the leader from the third before disputing it from the eighth, led when not fluent 3 out and, having been headed between the last 2, rallied to lead again final 100 yds, proving most game; she's a credit to connections who, just like last year, were fully rewarded in going for the big prize, in this case rather than the new mares' chase later in the week. **Nube Negra** saved for this since defeating Altior at Kempton over Christmas, took his form up further and didn't have things go ideally late on, though he probably wasn't closing quite quickly enough on the doughty winner to go as far as to call him an unlucky loser; patiently ridden, he'd crept closer by 4 out, was still going well when avoiding trouble after the next, was asked for his effort only after 2 out and, after pecking slightly at the last, was forced to switch on the run-in before running on, taking second in the final 50 yds and eroding the gap to the winner at the line; this was just his sixth run over fences, the potential there for him to do a bit better yet, easy to see him being primed for the Tingle Creek later in the year. **Chacun Pour Soi** who'd been forced to miss the race last year when suffering an abscess on the morning of the contest, arrived this time as the standout performer in the division, Put The Kettle On more than 8 lengths behind him at Christmas, but he couldn't land the one big prize that still eludes his trainer at this meeting, seemingly produced perfectly to win the race (having ensured a couple were majorly squeezed for room after 3 out when his rider secured the inside rail, a manoeuvre that probably should have resulted in a greater punishment than a 2-day careless riding ban) but unable to find any extra when required; chased leaders, took strong hold, not fluent water jump, produced to lead soon after 2 out, collared final 100 yds, found less than looked likely; this has to go down as a major opportunity missed, his task next year likely to be all the harder against the likes of Shishkin. **Greaneteen** only fourth in the Grand Annual last year, produced a career best, just as in the Tingle Creek looking fully at home at this level; held up, not fluent eighth, headway out wide when not fluent 3 out, loomed up approaching home turn, every chance 2 out, edged left run-in before carried back right by Nube Negra, kept on; he'll have the option of going up in trip for the Melling Chase or going back to Sandown for the Celebration. **Sceau Royal** produced a remarkable effort to finish as close as he did given quite how badly he was affected by the melee after 3 out, virtually on the floor and losing all momentum, while he met further congestion approaching the home turn and he simply has to go down as unlucky, looking in the form of his life in being beaten less than 4 lengths after all that, while his Newbury form was also franked by Greaneteen (a nod to Champ's chance in the Gold Cup). **First Flow** failed to repeat his Clarence House form, not looking comfortable going back left-handed, though to his credit having looked like dropping right out at one stage he did get himself back into contention; untidy third, not fluent sixth, tracked pace until next, firmly off pace when hung right after 4 out with Bass virtually on one rein all the way down the hill, progress again after 3 out, plugged on. **Notebook** on his toes beforehand but not worked up to the extent he was prior to the Arkle without the crowds this year, nonetheless still failed to give his running at this meeting for the third time, seemingly just not his track; settled mid-field, untidy 3 out, chased leaders soon after, faded from 2 out. **Cilaos Emery** was badly let down by his jumping in a championship race over fences, seemingly taken right out of his comfort zone from very early; soon behind, made mistakes, some headway approaching home turn and had got himself just about in touch when blundering 2 out, not recover. **Rouge Vif** failed to bounce back after 11 weeks off, already on the retreat when the scrimmaging after 3 out finished him off; led or disputed from third, clouted 4 out, weakening when badly hampered after next, dropped away home turn.

Weatherbys Champion Bumper (Standard Open National Hunt Flat) (Grade 1) (1)

Pos	Btn	Horse	Age	Wgt	Eq	Trainer	Jockey	SP
1		SIR GERHARD (IRE)	6	11-5		W. P. Mullins, Ireland	Rachael Blackmore	85/40
2	½	KILCRUIT (IRE)	6	11-5		W. P. Mullins, Ireland	P. Townend	10/11f
3	6½	ELLE EST BELLE	5	10-12		Dan Skelton	Harry Skelton	16/1
4	1¼	THREE STRIPE LIFE (IRE)	5	11-5		Mrs Denise Foster, Ireland	J. W. Kennedy	10/1
5	4½	SUPER SIX	4	10-12		Nigel Twiston-Davies	Tom Bellamy	80/1
6	¾	GRANGEE (FR)	5	10-12		W. P. Mullins, Ireland	D. E. Mullins	18/1
7	½	WONDERWALL (IRE)	5	11-5		Richard Spencer	James Bowen	50/1
8	2	RAMILLIES (IRE)	6	11-5		W. P. Mullins, Ireland	B. J. Cooper	14/1
9	3	I LIKE TO MOVE IT	4	10-12		Nigel Twiston-Davies	Sam Twiston-Davies	40/1
10	3½	SHEARER (IRE)	5	11-5	(t)	Paul Nicholls	A. P. Heskin	50/1
11	5	CHEMICAL ENERGY (IRE)	5	11-5		Mrs Denise Foster, Ireland	Robbie Power	50/1
12	5½	COOL JET (IRE)	5	11-5		W. P. Mullins, Ireland	B. Hayes	50/1
13	2¾	JACK'S A LEGEND	6	11-5		Alan Jones	Tom O'Brien	80/1
14	54	CREGGAN WHITE HARE (IRE)	6	11-5	(t)	Sean Conway	Jamie Bargary	300/1

14 ran Race Time 3m 55.20 Closing Sectional (3.90f): 53.9s (103.8%) Winning Owner: Cheveley Park Stud

For the second time in 3 runnings, a field of just 14 for the Champion Bumper, though this is more likely to be a blip than a trend, smaller fields in the Grade 1 novices having been a feature of the week, with the lack of social/speculative runners—the Spa on Friday the exception; the first 2 might well have been further along in their career but for the shutdown soon after last season's Festival, the runner-up making his debut later in March, the winner bought for £400,000 at the sale here the previous December, the price tag the obvious answer to anyone wondering why points rather than bumpers have become the focus of those looking to sell on young horses; the form of the first 2 is well up to the recent standards for the race, even if the contest overall lacked the depth usually associated with it; that said, physically this was a good field and the race seems sure to throw up plenty of winners over jumps next season; the winner added to Willie Mullins' remarkable record in the race, though in different circumstances he would have been the fourth winner of the week at the halfway point for Gordon Elliott; the early pace wasn't so good as it often is and the winner had the run of things under a well-judged ride, Rachael Blackmore completing a first—and last-race Grade 1 double after 3 spills in between. **Sir Gerhard** on first outing since leaving Gordon Elliott, got the perfect ride under the conditions and had just enough left to hold off the challenge of the runner-up, running to a very smart level, little between the first 2 in terms of ability and both top prospects for jumping, his physique very much that of a chaser, so perhaps a switch there rather than hurdling is an option, particularly given he's already 6; led, went with enthusiasm, kicked on before straight, clear 2f out, ridden over 1f out, edged right, ridden out; he followed Envoi Allen and Ferny Hollow in winning this race for the Cheveley Park Stud for the third year running. **Kilcruit** strong in the betting, didn't have the race set up for him in quite the same way as at Leopardstown, the winner getting first run on him; never far away, travelled well, effort home turn, still plenty to do over 1f out, kept on well, nearest at the finish; like the winner, he's a leading contender for novice hurdle honours next winter, though a switch straight to fences wouldn't be a first for one from this stable in this race. **Elle Est Belle** showed much improved form, ridden in very similar fashion to her first 2 wins, though such tactics probably weren't the optimum under these circumstances; in rear, travelled well, steady headway over 4f out, ridden straight, kept on well, took third near finish; she looks a useful prospect for novice hurdles next season. **Three Stripe Life** the only runner in the field to have contested just one race, shaped well in the circumstances, having plenty of stamina in his pedigree and under less testing conditions than those he faced on debut; mid-division, effort home turn, stayed on, made little impression; a useful prospect for novice hurdling next season. **Super Six** has a fair bit about him physically and acquited himself really well up in grade, particularly given he would clearly have benefited from more emphasis on stamina; held up, not settle fully, ridden over 3f out, stayed on over 1f out, nearest at the finish; he should win races next season, provided he's campaigned at a realistic level. **Grangee** ran respectably taking on geldings, though she's essentially a stayer and would have been better served by more of a test, taking too long to get going from a moderate position; held up, shaken up 4f out, not quicken, stayed on over 1f out, nearest at the finish; she lacks physique but will surely be placed to win races over hurdles next season. **Wonderwall** ran well upped in grade, though better positioned the way the race developed than a few that finished in front of him; prominent, shaken up over 3f out, not quicken entering straight. **Ramillies** looks the part and clearly ran better than last time, though his finishing effort left something to be desired, given how well positioned he was; tracked pace, travelled well, shaken up home turn, not quicken, edged left, weakened over 1f out. **I Like To Move It** was below form, this perhaps coming a bit soon after his run in a good race at Newbury; mid-field, took keen hold, labouring before straight. **Shearer** wasn't disgraced in first-time tongue strap, taking a big step up in class, though he backed out of things more readily than ideal; handy, pushed along over 3f out, soon done with. **Chemical Energy** has some filling out to do and again failed to repeat the form he showed in the autumn; mid-division, labouring over 3f out. **Cool Jet** was one of the best on looks but had plenty to find on form and failed to run even to the level he'd shown at Thurles; held up, not settle fully, some headway 4f out, weakened approaching straight. **Jack's A Legend** who'd had a breathing operation since last seen, looked out of his depth; held up, ridden 5f out, left behind soon after. **Creggan White Hare** had done nothing to suggest he had a chance at this level; held up, lost touch over 4f out, tailed off.

CHELTENHAM Thursday March 18
GOOD to SOFT

Marsh Novices' Chase (Golden Miller) (Grade 1) (1)

Pos	Btn	Horse	Age	Wgt	Eq	Trainer	Jockey	SP
1		CHANTRY HOUSE (IRE)	7	11-4		Nicky Henderson	Nico de Boinville	9/1
2	3	FUSIL RAFFLES (FR)	6	11-4		Nicky Henderson	Daryl Jacob	14/1
3	2	ASTERION FORLONGE (FR)	7	11-4	(t)	W. P. Mullins, Ireland	P. Townend	14/1
4	3	CHATHAM STREET LAD (IRE)	9	11-4		Michael Winters, Ireland	D. J. O'Keeffe	14/1
5	4	SHAN BLUE (IRE)	7	11-4		Dan Skelton	Harry Skelton	10/1
6	30	BLACKBOW (IRE)	8	11-4	(h+t)	W. P. Mullins, Ireland	B. J. Cooper	40/1
7	25	DARVER STAR (IRE)	9	11-4	(t)	Gavin Patrick Cromwell, Ireland	Keith Donoghue	33/1
F		ENVOI ALLEN (FR)	7	11-4	(t)	Henry de Bromhead, Ireland	J. W. Kennedy	4/9f

8 ran Race Time 5m 02.30 Closing Sectional (3.84f): 60.4s (97.3%) Winning Owner: Mr John P. McManus

The conveyor belt of short-priced favourites at this year's Festival continued with the switch to the New Course for Day 3, quite remarkable that the 3 Grade 1 novice chases this week all saw a horse sent off at 4/9 or shorter, though, unlike Shishkin and Monkfish before him, Envoi Allen fluffed his lines having looked such a sound jumper of fences to this point; his early departure shaped the race in more ways than one, the major injection of pace from Harry Skelton on Shan Blue as far out as halfway surely a direct consequence of the favourite's exit leaving a race firmly up for grabs, and that played into the hands of the more judiciously-ridden Henderson pair, the form rated as an average running of the race. **Chantry House** has met with defeat only twice under Rules, avenging the second of them with his stablemate Fusil Raffles from December on this less testing ground, also having had surgery on his back since then, benefiting from the fierce pace but that's not to put a cap on his potential necessarily, probably the best prospect for next season of those that finished the race regardless; chased leaders, not fluent ninth, shaken up eleventh, not fluent again next, effort approaching home turn, led soon after 2 out, in command after last, driven out; he leaves the impression that a step up in trip would be no bad thing at all, the Mildmay perhaps just as likely a target as the Manifesto were he to head to Aintree. **Fusil Raffles** had had Chantry House behind when scoring here on bad ground in December, but is at least as good away from the mud and ran really well, his rider wisely not getting embroiled in a battle with Shan Blue from halfway, his winning stablemate probably just the better longer-term prospect, even if he is a year older; jumped soundly, led until seventh, effort after 3 out, led again briefly next, edged left, pecked last, kept on; Aintree should suit him just as well. **Asterion Forlonge** had seemingly gained confidence in his jumping when well behind Monkfish at Leopardstown and saw that enabling him to get back on the up, creeping into contention from 4 out and trading odds on in-running when briefly seeming to be going best approaching the second last but edging left from there and unable to find any extra after he was untidy at the last. **Chatham Street Lad** back up in trip after 9 weeks off, looked comfortable at this level, as might have been expected from such a strong traveller, but found his jumping letting him down in the final third of the race, the less testing ground perhaps a factor in that; mid-division, went with zest, mistakes from eleventh, effort on inner home turn, forced to switch approaching 2 out, hung left flat, one paced. **Shan Blue** had good claims of coming out on top once Envoi Allen departed but saw his chance severely compromised by a ride that is best filed under the 'rush of blood' category, Skelton happy to take a lead from Fusil Raffles early on but, almost certainly influenced by the favourite's departure, injecting a huge amount of pace from as far out as halfway, Shan Blue understandably flagging late on; chased leader, led after seventh and immediately pressed on, not fluent next but still upped the ante further, steadied into 4 out and untidy there, reduced advantage approaching home turn, headed when not fluent 2 out, no extra, ridden too aggressively; Aintree should suit him but he did have a hard race here. **Blackbow** was never really in the hunt upped 3f in trip; dropped out, hampered fourth, steadied into 4 out, no threat after, not persevered with once held; perhaps he'll be better off ridden more prominently again. **Darver Star** a close second to Honeysuckle in last year's Irish Champion Hurdle and placed in the Champion Hurdle, lacks size and substance, outclassed physically in this field, and is unlikely to prove as good in this sphere as over hurdles, though his chance here was all but over when Envoi Allen fell in front of him, having to hurdle that one and not jumping with any confidence thereafter, losing touch from the eighth and eased after 4 out; perhaps a return to hurdling is in store, even if the prospect of taking on Honeysuckle at Punchestown isn't a particularly attractive one. **Envoi Allen** suffered the first bump in a road that many believe will lead right to the top of the sport, impossible to know if he'd been affected by the high-profile recent stable change but, having been very laid-back in the preliminaries, was less so once at the start and took a slightly keener hold than usual in the race, coming up quite long at the second and paying the price when doing likewise at the fourth; this doesn't dent his enormous potential, and will hopefully prove a one-off.

Ryanair Chase (Festival Trophy) (Grade 1) (1)

Pos	Btn	Horse	Age	Wgt	Eq	Trainer	Jockey	SP
1		ALLAHO (FR)	7	11-10	(t)	W. P. Mullins, Ireland	Rachael Blackmore	3/1f
2	12	FAKIR D'OUDAIRIES (FR)	6	11-10		Joseph Patrick O'Brien, Ireland	M. P. Walsh	11/2
3	½	TORNADO FLYER (IRE)	8	11-10		W. P. Mullins, Ireland	D. E. Mullins	25/1
4	6	KALASHNIKOV (IRE)	8	11-10	(s+t)	Amy Murphy	Jack Quinlan	25/1
5	35	FANION D'ESTRUVAL (FR)	6	11-10		Venetia Williams	Charlie Deutsch	66/1
pu		CHRIS'S DREAM (IRE)	9	11-10		Henry de Bromhead, Ireland	Robbie Power	28/1
pu		IMPERIAL AURA (IRE)	8	11-10	(t)	Kim Bailey	David Bass	8/1
pu		MELON	9	11-10	(s)	W. P. Mullins, Ireland	B. J. Cooper	8/1
pu		MIN (FR)	10	11-10		W. P. Mullins, Ireland	P. Townend	4/1

pu	MISTER FISHER (IRE)	7	11-10		Nicky Henderson	Nico de Boinville	8/1
pu	SAMCRO (IRE)	9	11-10	(t)	Mrs Denise Foster, Ireland	J. W. Kennedy	15/2

11 ran   Race Time 5m 10.10   Closing Sectional (3.84f): 59.30s (97.6%)   Winning Owner: Cheveley Park Stud

With odds-on favourites – and a maximum field size of 8 – in each of the Grade 1 novice chases at this year's Festival the dilution of races at the top level of the NH game has understandably been a hot topic in recent days but, rather ironically, the Ryanair, which has at times been seen as something of an excuse for connections to dodge the Champion Chase or Gold Cup, provided both the line-up and spectacle of the week, Min facing no shortage of opposition—most of them genuine 2½m horses—as he attempted to defend his crown, including 3 of the first 4 home from the 2020 Golden Miller as well as the Arkle second Fakir d'Oudairies and upwardly-mobile Imperial Aura, though in the event the race was about one horse and one horse only, Allaho simply in a different league from an early stage; after a false start there was a rush for the lead, Allaho and Min soon racing clear of the main pack, going a gallop which took the majority out of their comfort zones, several making mistakes, the stragglers closing up a bit after 5 out before Allaho turned the screw again after the next, Min crying enough after the third last, his younger stable companion having the race in the bag entering the straight, the performance—which was backed up by the clock—rated right up with the 2 previous best winners of the race, Cue Card in 2013 and Vautour in 2016. **Allaho** third at the last 2 Festivals when running over 3m, charged off in front over this shorter trip and didn't look vulnerable at any point, a string of high-class chasers left trailing in his wake, utter domination, a first-time tongue strap seemingly doing something to facilitate this top class performance, some pretty rapid consolation for his owners after Envoi Allen's earlier fall; forced pace and jumped superbly, tanked along, steadied the gallop briefly after 5 out, drew clear again from 3 out and in command entering straight, shaken up between last 2, driven out; aggressive rides over this intermediate trip might prove to be just what's needed to bring out the very best in him. **Fakir d'Oudairies** was well backed returning to 2½m and did just about best of the rest, runner-up to a top-notcher for the second time in as many starts; mid-field, not fluent sixth, tenth, ridden 3 out, went third early in straight, stayed on but never a match for the winner. **Tornado Flyer** back up in trip, returned to something like his best though was never actually competitive from a win perspective; raced off the pace going a bit in snatches, not fluent tenth, outpaced 3 out, went fourth 2 out, stayed on to take third after the last. **Kalashnikov** back in cheekpieces and in a first-time tongue strap, outran his odds despite not looking entirely comfortable with the strong gallop, losing second only after the last; mid-field, outpaced, some headway twelfth, went second home turn, no extra after last. **Fanion d'Estruval** was out of his depth, basically ridden to get around; in rear, mistakes tenth, 5 out, never involved. **Chris's Dream** seemed to find this a shock to the system after 3 months off, one of the first beaten; raced off the pace, clouted sixth, struggling after eighth. **Imperial Aura** easy to back after 10 weeks off, was in trouble a fair way out, subsequently found to have bled from the nose; in touch, lost place tenth, awkward next, weakened. **Melon** back in headgear, disappointed for the first time at the Festival, taken off his feet in a strongly-run race back down in trip; mid-field, lost ground tenth, hit eleventh, beaten after. **Min** looked back in form for a long way, which made his finishing effort all the more disappointing, even considering he raced closer to Allaho—who he'd beaten at a murky Punchestown in December—than any of the others, folding soon after 3 out; he's got a bit to prove all of a sudden. **Mister Fisher** after 3 months off, was in contention for longer than most but was ultimately let down by his jumping; in touch, travelled well, left back leg in the water jump (ninth), not fluent twelfth, blundered 3 out, not recover. **Samcro** last year's Golden Miller winner, shaped quite similarly to at Leopardstown over Christmas, a big disappointment since his reappearance; mid-field, lost place when clouted seventh, struggling after next and pulled up quite quickly.

Paddy Power Stayers' Hurdle (Grade 1) (1)

Pos	Btn	Horse	Age	Wgt	Eq	Trainer	Jockey	SP
1		FLOORING PORTER (IRE)	6	11-10	(t)	Gavin Patrick Cromwell, Ireland	D. E. Mullins	12/1
2	3¼	SIRE DU BERLAIS (FR)	9	11-10	(b+t)	Mrs Denise Foster, Ireland	M. P. Walsh	5/1
3	1¾	PAISLEY PARK (IRE)	9	11-10		Emma Lavelle	Aidan Coleman	9/4f
4	½	BEACON EDGE (IRE)	7	11-10		Noel Meade, Ireland	Sean Flanagan	10/1
5	3½	THE STORYTELLER (IRE)	10	11-10		Mrs Denise Foster, Ireland	Keith Donoghue	11/1
6	4¼	VINNDICATION (IRE)	8	11-10	(s+t)	Kim Bailey	David Bass	16/1
7	8½	BACARDYS (FR)	10	11-10	(t)	W. P. Mullins, Ireland	P. Townend	50/1
8	5½	YOUNEVERCALL (IRE)	10	11-10	(s+t)	Kim Bailey	Ciaran Gethings	100/1
9	2¾	IF THE CAP FITS (IRE)	9	11-10	(s+t)	Harry Fry	Daryl Jacob	25/1
F		LISNAGAR OSCAR (IRE)	8	11-10		Rebecca Curtis	Harry Skelton	11/1
pu		FURY ROAD (IRE)	7	11-10	(t)	Mrs Denise Foster, Ireland	J. W. Kennedy	4/1
pu		LIL ROCKERFELLER (USA)	10	11-10	(v)	Neil King	Bryony Frost	66/1
pu		MAIN FACT (USA)	8	11-10	(b)	David Pipe	Fergus Gillard	150/1
pu		RESERVE TANK (IRE)	7	11-10		Colin Tizzard	Robbie Power	50/1
pu		SAM SPINNER	9	11-10	(b)	Jedd O'Keeffe	Henry Brooke	66/1

15 ran Race Time 5m 52.30 Closing Sectional (3.7f): 55.9s (97.3%) Winning Owner: Flooring Porter Syndicate

Perhaps not quite of Allaho proportions, but a pretty staggering performance in its own right, the winner setting a gallop considerably quicker than in the Pertemps Final a little over an hour earlier yet never really looking like being overhauled, such a display even more remarkable considering he was beaten in a handicap from a mark of 131 as recently as October; some of the competition was removed when last year's winner fell soon after halfway, badly hampering the well-backed Fury Road, putting a slight limitation on the form, but all of the other main contenders had a chance of sorts from 2 out; ante-post favourite Thyme Hill had been ruled out of the race the week before, offering a crumb of comfort for British racing fans faced with a largely Irish-dominated finish in a division which, since Big Buck's, has been very even, this incidentally one of 5 races on the day in which at least the first 2 home were trained in Ireland. **Flooring Porter** has improved out of all recognition, winning his first handicap from a mark of just 105 and beaten in one from a mark of 131 as recently as October yet now looking potentially the dominant staying hurdler, such was the brazen way he grabbed this prize, setting a gallop considerably quicker than in the Pertemps Final earlier on the card yet never really looking susceptible to the finishers, all achieved under a rider who was called up only earlier in the day, too, regular partner Jonathan Moore declaring himself unfit to take the ride following a fall at Naas the previous weekend; made all, jumped well, travelled fluently, still going well entering straight, brought towards stand rail but wanted to lug back left, in control when jinked after last, kept going well; has plenty of time on his side as a 6-y-o, though his style isn't exactly reminiscent of those that have dominated this division this century, and perhaps not one renowned for longevity. **Sire du Berlais** so well suited to this C&D, ran at least as well as when landing his second Pertemps Final 12 months earlier, closing the gap on Flooring Porter from the Leopardstown Christmas Hurdle but finding that

3-year-younger rival improving too much for him to overhaul; hampered slightly start, mid-division, untidy third, effort from 3 out, took second run-in, stayed on but no real impression on winner; like so many from his yard, he's become a real Festival stalwart, also placed in the Martin Pipe before those 2 Pertemps Final wins. **Paisley Park** bidding to become the first since Inglis Drever to regain the Stayers' Hurdle crown, briefly seemed to get motoring turning for home in a manner similar to the surge that had taken him to the front 2 years earlier (trading as low as 1.58 in-running) but couldn't find an extra gear, perhaps suffering from the cancellation of the Cleeve Hurdle, meaning this was his first run in 13 weeks, possibly set to improve a little for it should he go to Aintree or Punchestown, though neither course is likely to suit him as well as this one; held up, untidy at the seventh where he was also hampered, pushed along before 3 out, made some headway out wide next and threatened entering straight but one paced latter stages, taking third only near finish. **Beacon Edge** is still firmly on the up and shaped a bit better than the bare result, not quite relaxing well enough on this first try at 3m to see the race out as well as dour stayers Sire du Berlais and Paisley Park, both of whom passed him only on the run-in after he'd looked the biggest threat to the winner from the point he'd moved into second crossing 2 out; he's got the option of going chasing next season. **The Storyteller** has held his form tremendously well over the past 15 months or so, a real credit to his yard, and he gave another very good account of himself, particularly as it was subsequently reported that he'd struck into himself; held up, hampered seventh, not fluent next, in contention 2 out, hung left early in straight, plugged on without being unduly punished. **Vinndication** after 4 months off, performed very creditably on what was just his fourth run over hurdles, his first in over 3 years, and it showed early on, possible that he'll do even better for this experience as a result; raced wide, handy, slow first and took time to adjust to jumping hurdles, close up still 2 out, one paced straight. **Bacardys** under Townend this year as the sole Mullins representative, was ridden every bit as patiently as previously in the race, firmly off the pace 3 out and still with plenty to do after the next, meeting some trouble approaching the home turn and unable to find any extra when asked for his effort in the straight; now 10, this was a stronger renewal than the one in which he'd finished third 12 months earlier and he has just a listed hurdle success to his name over the past 4 seasons. **Younevercall** shaped better than the distance beaten suggests after 10 weeks off, though a tame finish on the back of yet another breathing operation, his third in the space of 5 runs, is a cause for concern, even were he to head back for the Sandown race on the final day of the season he won in 2019; chased leaders, yet to be asked for effort when untidy 2 out, not quicken from there, weakened early in straight. **If The Cap Fits** sporting a first-time tongue strap and refitted with cheekpieces for this return to hurdling after a stuttering attempt at chasing, found this too competitive, probably not the force of old at the age of 9; mid-field, not fluent fourth, pushed along after 3 out, untidy next, left behind. **Lisnagar Oscar** bidding to defend his crown under a new rider, seemed to have got into a good rhythm tracking the pace when falling heavily at the seventh, turning a somersault and also canoned into by one of those behind, hopefully none the worse. **Fury Road** was clearly fancied to overturn Leopardstown Christmas Hurdle form with Flooring Porter and Sire du Berlais given the amount of money for him, and it's easy to put a line through this, the effort of getting back into the race after he was seriously impeded by Lisnagar Oscar's fall leaving him with nothing left late on; raced wide, held up, not fluent fourth, badly hampered seventh, crept closer after 3 out, effort after next, weakened, pulled up last. **Lil Rockerfeller** in first-time visor after 9 weeks off, shaped as if he might have been amiss, notwithstanding this level of competition is too hot for him these days, a full 4 years since he was touched off in the race; close up, not fluent first, lost ground 3 out, faltered and eased soon after. **Main Fact** never figured in first-time blinkers; in rear, hampered seventh, mistake 3 out, labouring after, behind when mistake again next. **Reserve Tank** had plenty on his plate but ran no sort of race even so; raced well off the pace, pushed along early final circuit, struggling when hampered seventh, never a threat. **Sam Spinner** in first-time blinkers after 4 months off, is a mere shadow of the horse who was sent off 9/4 for this in 2018, or the one who finished second to Paisley Park 12 months later; slowly into stride and had to be rousted early, in touch, made mistakes, lost place before 3 out, beaten quickly after the worst of his errors there.

CHELTENHAM Friday March 19
GOOD to SOFT

JCB Triumph Hurdle (Grade 1) (1)

Pos	Btn	Horse	Age	Wgt	Eq	Trainer	Jockey	SP
1		QUILIXIOS	4	11-0		Henry de Bromhead, Ireland	Rachael Blackmore	2/1
2	3¼	ADAGIO (GER)	4	11-0		David Pipe	Tom Scudamore	10/1
3	hd	HAUT EN COULEURS (FR)	4	11-0		W. P. Mullins, Ireland	P. Townend	20/1
4	1¼	ZANAHIYR (IRE)	4	11-0	(t)	Mrs Denise Foster, Ireland	J. W. Kennedy	11/8f
5	11	TRITONIC	4	11-0		Alan King	A. P. Heskin	4/1
6	9	TAX FOR MAX (GER)	4	11-0	(h)	W. P. Mullins, Ireland	Daryl Jacob	33/1
7	14	TALKING ABOUT YOU	4	10-7		Sean Curran	Harry Bannister	125/1
8	3	HISTORIC HEART (IRE)	4	11-0	(v)	Nigel Hawke	David Noonan	125/1

8 ran Race Time 4m 06.80 Closing Sectional (3.7f): 51.7s (105.1%) Winning Owner: Cheveley Park Stud

The smallest field for the Triumph Hurdle since the first Cheltenham running in 1965, when 7 went to post, though in common with the Baring Bingham and the Supreme the race lacked only in numbers, the best in the field going into it having form not far off the recent standard for winners of the contest—not including Goshen's performance, obviously—and though Zanahiyr wasn't quite at his best and Tritonic flopped, the form still looks well up to scratch, the race run at a sound pace and with no obvious hard-luck stories. **Quilixios** progressed again on first outing since leaving Gordon Elliott, establishing himself as the best in the division, though there are grounds for thinking the third and fourth might give him a tougher race another day; close up, jumped fluently, travelled strongly, upsides third, led 2 out, quickened straight, looked in control last, had bit in hand; he's not the most taking sort but is open to further improvement. **Adagio** ran at least as well as when successful at Chepstow, his record a fine one in his first season, presumably the Anniversary next on the agenda, likely to go well again in that, even if he doesn't appeal as having the longer term potential of a couple of the others; in touch, effort after 2 out, challenged approaching last, kept on run-in, no match for winner. **Haut En Couleurs** successful in a newcomers hurdle for Gabriel Leenders at Auteuil in October, belied his lack of experience, running a race full of promise, probably as good a prospect as there is in this field, unlike the other principals bred for jumping; held up, took keen hold, effort after 2 out, chased leader approaching last, kept on; sure to progress and win more races, looks one to follow. **Zanahiyr** in first-time tongue strap (somewhat worryingly), wasn't in quite the same form as when so impressive on his last 2 starts, not seeming quite so sharp after a 3-month break; handy, jumped fluently, travelled well, shaken up home turn, not quicken, kept on run-in; he'd looked so good previously, with form that stacks up, that he may well be able to better this if he turns up at Aintree or Punchestown. **Tritonic** was disappointing, given the level of his Flat form and the style of his wins on his first 2 starts over hurdles, even if the Adonis form is perhaps not so good as it seemed; waited with, shaken up 2 out, not quicken entering straight. **Tax For Max** was set a stiff task for just his second start over hurdles and still looks a work in progress in this discipline, needing to learn to settle for a start; dropped out, refused to settle, effort 2 out, made little impression; his Flat form suggests he could improve a fair bit if he can adapt to running over hurdles better. **Talking About You** has done really well this season but this was a step too far; led, jinked approaching 2 out, headed there, soon done with. **Historic Heart** in a change of headgear, was simply out of his depth; held up, not fluent second, labouring before 2 out.

Albert Bartlett Novices' Hurdle (Spa) (Grade 1) (1)

Pos	Btn	Horse	Age	Wgt	Eq	Trainer	Jockey	SP
1		VANILLIER (FR)	6	11-5	(t)	Gavin Patrick Cromwell, Ireland	M. P. Walsh	14/1
2	11	OSCAR ELITE (IRE)	6	11-5	(t)	Colin Tizzard	Jonjo O'Neill Jr.	40/1
3	1½	STREETS OF DOYEN (IRE)	7	11-5	(s)	John McConnell, Ireland	S. D. Torrens	10/1
4	2¾	STATTLER (IRE)	6	11-5		W. P. Mullins, Ireland	P. Townend	7/2f
5	¾	ALAPHILIPPE (IRE)	7	11-5		Fergal O'Brien	Paddy Brennan	11/1
6	nk	THREEUNDERTHRUFIVE (IRE)	6	11-5		Paul Nicholls	A. P. Heskin	11/1
7	1½	CHAMPAGNESUPEROVER (IRE)	6	11-5	(t)	Olly Murphy	Aidan Coleman	100/1
8	2	TORYGRAPH (IRE)	6	11-5	(s)	Mrs Denise Foster, Ireland	J. W. Kennedy	7/1
9	2	N'GOLO (IRE)	6	11-5	(h+t)	W. P. Mullins, Ireland	D. E. Mullins	40/1
10	11	FAKIERA (FR)	6	11-5	(s)	Mrs Denise Foster, Ireland	Keith Donoghue	4/1
11	7½	BARBADOS BUCK'S (IRE)	6	11-5		Paul Nicholls	Harry Cobden	8/1
12	13	THE COB (IRE)	7	11-5		Ben Pauling	Daryl Jacob	28/1
13	2¼	PATS FANCY (IRE)	6	11-5		Rebecca Curtis	Rachael Blackmore	28/1
14	½	ASK A HONEY BEE (IRE)	7	11-5	(s)	Fergal O'Brien	Richard Patrick	80/1
pu		ADRIMEL (FR)	6	11-5	(s+t)	Tom Lacey	Richard Johnson	9/1
pu		BEATTHEBULLET (IRE)	7	11-5	(s)	Rebecca Curtis	Harry Skelton	200/1

16 ran Race Time 6m 01.80 Closing Sectional (3.7f): 55.4s (100.8%) Winning Owner: Mrs H. M. Keaveney

While the Triumph and the other Grade 1 novices had seen a much smaller number of runners than typical line up, the Spa had its usual double-figure field, perhaps because it looked an open and rather substandard division, though it proved neither in the event, the winner clearly a class apart and much improved for a sound pace and less testing ground at 3m, his winning margin the widest since the race was promoted to Grade 1 in 2008, Wichita Lineman scoring by 12 lengths the previous year, though the form shown by Vanillier looks no better than that achieved by Minella Indo and Monkfish in gaining much narrower successes in the last 2 renewals, something to live up to in following in their footsteps. **Vanillier** away from the mud, showed much improved form, clearly relishing this rather different test; pressed leader, tanked along, led when not fluent first, went on 2 out, quickened clear approaching last, well on top finish; he has a lot to live up, given the most recent winners of this race, but now that he has found his right conditions he looks open to further improvement. **Oscar Elite** in first-time tongue strap and back up markedly in trip, put a couple of disappointing efforts behind him, indeed showed much improved form, clearly after all the useful prospect he'd looked in winning at Chepstow; in touch, travelled well, headway before 2 out, chased leader approaching last, kept on, no impression on winner; he has the physique for fences, the pedigree too, and will be an interesting proposition for novice chasing next season. **Streets of Doyen** with cheekpieces retained, was quickly back to form, returned to a much more suitable trip, confirming himself a useful staying novice; held up, good progress before 2 out, ridden after, stayed on straight, went third run-in. **Stattler** looked the form pick on his third at Leopardstown, though that left him short of the standard usually required to win this and he failed to match it, never mind better it, stepped up in trip; handy, travelled well, ridden after 2 out, keeping on when mistake last, no extra; he's not an obvious chaser on looks, in contrast to plenty in this field. **Alaphilippe** ran creditably, up in grade, looking a thorough stayer, longer-distance events over fences surely his future; held up, effort approaching 2 out, outpaced after, rallied approaching last, stayed on, nearest at the finish. **Threeunderthrufive** as good looking a sort as there was in the line-up, very much a future chaser, ran respectably up in class, just lacking a turn of foot; close up early, settled mid-field, blundered seventh, shaken up 2 out, not quicken, stayed on run-in. **Champagnesuperover** upped markedly in trip, ran well upped in grade, exaggerated tactics over the longer trip understandable but possibly not ideal; dropped out, travelled well, still plenty to do 2 out, ridden after, headway early in straight, hung left run-in, no extra final 100 yds. **Torygraph** was below form in first-time cheekpieces, away from the mud and in a strong race, reason enough why he performed as he did; close up first, settled mid-field, ridden after 3 out, left behind after next. **N'golo** upped markedly in trip, in first-time hood, ran much better than the last twice, though he looked far from straightforward, doubtful whether he wants this sort of trip as well; handy, refused to settle, ridden after 2 out, hung badly left early in straight, weakened approaching last. **Fakiera** away from the mud, went better through the race than is typical, though ironically he didn't finish the race nearly so well as he usually does; never far away, travelled well, mistake eighth, shaken up after 2 out, weakened early in straight. **Barbados Buck's** seemed likely to benefit from a proper test of stamina, but proved rather disappointing, his stable having a pretty quiet week; held up, took keen hold, pushed along briefly circuit out, never on terms; he's likely to go chasing next season, and will be placed to advantage in that sphere for a stable that is in a class of its own in Britain away from this meeting. **The Cob** had been supplemented for this after his surprise win at Doncaster, but it proved not money well spent, in nothing like the same form under less testing conditions; held up, pushed along 3 out, left behind next. **Pats Fancy** essentially found this too competitive, finishing well held; close up, led second, headed after third, ridden 3 out, weakened soon after; he has the look of a chaser. **Ask A Honey Bee** in first-time cheekpieces, turned in a lacklustre display, for all that he had a stiff task at this level; shaken up halfway, always behind. **Adrimel** upped in trip, folded quickly after matching strides with the winner until 2 out; prominent, led after third, headed 2 out, weakened early in straight, pulled up last; he has the look of a chaser and remains a useful prospect longer term. **Beatthebullet** faced a stiff task in this grade; mid-division, ridden after 3 out, soon done with, pulled up straight.

Wellchild Cheltenham Gold Cup Chase (Grade 1) (1)

Pos	Btn	Horse	Age	Wgt	Eq	Trainer	Jockey	SP
1		MINELLA INDO (IRE)	8	11-10		Henry de Bromhead, Ireland	J. W. Kennedy	9/1
2	1¼	A PLUS TARD (FR)	7	11-10	(t)	Henry de Bromhead, Ireland	Rachael Blackmore	10/3
3	4¼	AL BOUM PHOTO (FR)	9	11-10		W. P. Mullins, Ireland	P. Townend	9/4f
4	24	NATIVE RIVER (IRE)	11	11-10	(b)	Colin Tizzard	Richard Johnson	12/1
5	4¼	FRODON (FR)	9	11-10	(t)	Paul Nicholls	Bryony Frost	16/1

6	15	ROYALE PAGAILLE (FR)	7	11-10		Venetia Williams	Charlie Deutsch	14/1
7	3	BLACK OP (IRE)	10	11-10	(s+t)	Tom George	Tom Scudamore	125/1
8	½	ASO (FR)	11	11-10	(s)	Venetia Williams	Daryl Jacob	150/1
9	33	KEMBOY (FR)	9	11-10		W. P. Mullins, Ireland	D. E. Mullins	16/1
pu		CHAMP (IRE)	9	11-10		Nicky Henderson	Nico de Boinville	13/2
pu		LOSTINTRANSLATION (IRE)	9	11-10	(t)	Colin Tizzard	Robbie Power	40/1
pu		SANTINI	9	11-10	(v)	Nicky Henderson	Aidan Coleman	12/1

12 ran Race Time 6m 45.30 Closing Sectional (3.84f): 57.60s (102.7%) Winning Owner: Mr Barry Maloney

The blue riband of steeplechasing, drawing a really representative field, the winners of the King George, Savills Chase and Irish Gold Cup in the line-up, as well as those that had run well in the race before, the winner of the last 2 years, the winner the year before that and the second and third from 2020, the first 2 in the final RSA Chase and a novice that had shown high-class form in handicaps flying the flag for the up-and-coming brigade, all plausible contenders for a Gold Cup that on paper was more open than the market suggested; the race was run at a sound gallop, though Frodon's jumping in front tested plenty of his rivals, the winner the one of those behind that jumped best, good jumps at the last 2 ensuring he maintained his advantage as the first 3, Irish-trained inevitably, drew well clear, the form shown by Minella Indo behind only Don Cossack among winners in the last decade; it was, above all, an engrossing horserace to watch, encapsulating everything jumping is about and it capped a week where the level of performance was consistently high. **Minella Indo** winner of the Spa Hurdle in 2019 and edged out by Champ in the RSA last season, proved better than ever back at this track, bouncing back from a couple of reverses when a short price at Leopardstown on his last 2 starts, always in a good rhythm and jumping as well as any bar Frodon; never far away, jumped well in main, travelled strongly, not fluent ninth, went second seventeenth, led soon after 3 out, ridden out; he's one of the best winners of this race in the last decade and is young enough to build further on his already excellent record. **A Plus Tard** winner of the novice handicap chase and third in the Ryanair at the last 2 Festivals, took his form up a notch further, tackling the longest trip he's yet faced, fine margins between him and his stable companion, caught briefly in a pocket as Black Op began to weaken, not so quick as the winner over the last 2 fences when a better jump was needed to get on terms; held up, jumped slightly right at times, travelled well, headway when mistake sixteenth, short of room after 4 out, chased leader home turn, held only final 100 yds; he's a year younger than the winner and only just arriving at the top of the staying chasing tree, further good races surely going to be added to his record. **Al Boum Photo** bidding to join Cottage Rake, Arkle and Best Mate as a 3-time winner of the Cheltenham Gold Cup, fell short in the attempt, though he probably ran to a very similar level to that of his wins, just beaten by better horses, though his jumping was a bit fiddly at times; in touch, not always fluent, travelled well, tracked pace approaching 3 out, short of room home turn, not quicken; he may well be back for a fourth attempt in 2022, all being well, though it's over 20 years since a horse as old as 10 won the race. **Native River** was far from disgraced, making the frame in the race for the fourth time, though his best chance of a second win in the race was perhaps last year's, which he missed, the conditions here just not placing enough emphasis on stamina, rather like in 2019 never really on the bridle, his finishing position owing plenty to his rider; chased leaders, uncomfortable with pace, ridden thirteenth, lost place fifteenth, rallied well straight, took fourth close home; he would have been a really interesting runner in the Grand National, but wasn't entered, the Bowl the option at Aintree, testing ground the key to his chance, should he go there. **Frodon** has a tremendous record at Cheltenham and his usual tactics were executed as well as they could have been, but he didn't get home over a trip that had threatened to be too far for him; led, jumped superbly, went with zest, headed after 3 out, soon done with, lost fourth close home; presumably the Bowl at Aintree is an option next, likely to be more competitive there, though the Oaksey Chase at Sandown might be ideal. **Royale Pagaille** running here in preference to either the Broadway or the NH Chase, found this much more challenging than handicap company and his jumping didn't really hold up as a result; held up, jumped sketchily, blundered seventeenth, labouring after, never on terms; may be best on soft/heavy ground as well. **Black Op** in first-time cheekpieces, was overfaced again and finished well held, though he showed up well for a long way, suggesting he'd be competitive at a more realistic level; close up, not fluent eleventh, pushed along fourteenth, weakened 3 out. **Aso** twice placed in the Ryanair, hasn't looked the force of old this season and was well held, though he shaped better than the distances indicate, a significant mistake as things were hotting up his undoing; held up, still plenty to do but yet to be asked for effort when blundered 4 out, ridden after and left behind. **Kemboy** was well held, this not really his track, for all he avoided the serious mistakes he's made here previously; close up, not always fluent, travelled well, weakened seventeenth; there's every chance he'll bounce back at Punchestown. **Champ** had beaten the winner (and Allaho) in the RSA last season and had shaped very well in his trial, over just 2m, but his race here was over as soon as it had begun, belting the first and never recovering, his rider calling it a day after barely a mile; held up, jumped badly, ridden after third, pulled up before seventh; he has the ability to make an impact at a high level, whether he can get back on track in what's left of the season after this remains to be seen. **Lostintranslation** third last season, has looked a shadow of that horse all winter, and although he took the eye beforehand he failed to revive; waited with, pushed along early final circuit, mistake eighteenth, labouring after, pulled up straight. **Santini** in a change of headgear (visor instead of cheekpieces) in a bid to get him back to the form that saw him finish runner-up last season, lost his chance with an awful mistake at the second ditch, though his attitude again looked very questionable and his temperament is clearly under suspicion; in touch, bad mistake seventh, mistake next, lost place, pulled up circuit out, turned it in; he's the one Grand National entry in the field, though there would be wiser options for his next run.

AINTREE Thursday April 8
GOOD to SOFT

Betway Bowl Chase (Grade 1) (1)

Pos	Btn	Horse	Age	Wgt	Eq	Trainer	Jockey	SP
1		CLAN DES OBEAUX (FR)	9	11-7	(s)	Paul Nicholls	Harry Cobden	5/2f
2	26	CLONDAW CASTLE (IRE)	9	11-7		Tom George	Jonathan Burke	13/2
3	18	NATIVE RIVER (IRE)	11	11-7	(b)	Colin Tizzard	Jonjo O'Neill Jr.	4/1
4	48	TIGER ROLL (IRE)	11	11-7	(b+t)	Mrs Denise Foster, Ireland	J. W. Kennedy	8/1
5	11	ASO (FR)	11	11-7	(s)	Venetia Williams	Charlie Deutsch	28/1
ur		MISTER FISHER (IRE)	7	11-7		Nicky Henderson	Nico de Boinville	15/2
pu		MILITARIAN	11	11-7		Andrew Martin	Mr James Martin	250/1
pu		REAL STEEL (FR)	8	11-7	(t)	Paul Nicholls	Bryony Frost	28/1
pu		WAITING PATIENTLY (IRE)	10	11-7	(s)	Ruth Jefferson	Brian Hughes	4/1

9 ran Race Time 6m 27.20 Closing Sectional (3.15f): 45.6s (107.2%) Winning Owner: Mr&Mrs P.K.Barber,G.Mason,Sir A Ferguson

Plenty had doubts about them beforehand and the chances are that only the winner gave its running, enough known about him to suggest he hasn't suddenly found 20 lb of improvement for the fitting of cheekpieces; a good pace proved too much for most. **Clan des Obeaux** was revitalised in first-time cheekpieces, though it's far more likely that he was the only one to give his running, rather than he found 20 lb improvement, the second time he's won a Grade 1 by more than 20 lengths, though on the first occasion too he was against opposition that rather fell apart; chased leader, travelled well, left in front twelfth, clear before 4 out, shaken up after 2 out, well clear soon after. **Clondaw Castle** was the only threat to the winner in the straight and is clearly in good form, though he ran out of steam late on, suggesting the trip stretched him; in touch, travelled well, headway end of back straight, chased leader 4 out, ridden approaching 2 out, left behind by winner soon after. **Native River** looked to be feeling the effects of a tough race at Cheltenham, not going at any stage after again failing to get away in front; in touch, ridden at start, went prominent fifth, outpaced before 4 out, lost second there, left behind straight; he looked really good at Sandown and hasn't had the same ground since, though his age is against his making an impact at the highest level next season. **Tiger Roll** easy to back, was well held faced with an unsuitable test, the stewards enquiring into his performance, noting connections' lengthy explanations; chased leaders early, mistake third, lost ground fifth, no chance early final circuit; it's hard to know what to expect from him next time. **Aso** ran no sort of race, perhaps still feeling the effects of his run at Cheltenham; soon behind, mistake sixth, labouring badly soon after, tailed off back straight. **Mister Fisher** upped in trip, departed too soon to stay what would have happened, though he went with more zest than most; led, took keen hold, blundered eleventh, unseated rider twelfth. **Militarian** faced a stiff task in this grade and wasn't up to it, though he shaped better than most, certainly as if in better form than being pulled up would indicate; held up, good progress seventh, blundered thirteenth, ridden after, weakened before 3 out, slow there, pulled up. **Real Steel** ran no sort of race after 3 months off, his last 2 runs clearly suggesting an issue of some sort; soon behind, never travelling well, pulled up straight. **Waiting Patiently** back up markedly in trip, ran one of his lesser races, not going that well from quite an early stage, not much of a surprise that he would perform like this, given his recent record; held up, mistakes first and eleventh, steady headway leaving back straight, ridden straight, found little, pulled up before last.

Betway Aintree Hurdle (Grade 1) (1)

Pos	Btn	Horse	Age	Wgt	Eq	Trainer	Jockey	SP
1		ABACADABRAS (FR)	7	11-7	(t)	Mrs Denise Foster, Ireland	J. W. Kennedy	5/1
2	1¼	BUZZ (FR)	7	11-7		Nicky Henderson	James Bowen	22/1
3	2¼	MILLERS BANK	7	11-7		Alex Hales	Kielan Woods	80/1
4	1¼	BUVEUR D'AIR (FR)	10	11-7		Nicky Henderson	Nico de Boinville	6/1
5	3¼	BREWIN'UPASTORM (IRE)	8	11-7	(t)	Olly Murphy	Aidan Coleman	15/2
6	hd	SILVER STREAK (IRE)	8	11-7		Evan Williams	Tom O'Brien	14/1
7	1½	NOT SO SLEEPY	9	11-7		Hughie Morrison	Jonathan Burke	20/1
8	1¼	MCFABULOUS (IRE)	7	11-7		Paul Nicholls	Harry Cobden	9/2
9	43	BALLYANDY	10	11-7		Nigel Twiston-Davies	Sam Twiston-Davies	50/1
ur		JASON THE MILITANT (IRE)	7	11-7	(t)	Henry de Bromhead, Ireland	Rachael Blackmore	3/1f
pu		SONG FOR SOMEONE (GER)	6	11-7		Tom Symonds	David Bass	15/2

11 ran Race Time 4m 59.00 Closing Sectional (3.15f): 45.5s (103.5%) Winning Owner: Gigginstown House Stud

A competitive renewal on paper, though quite a few had their stamina to prove and ultimately it probably didn't make up into the sum of its parts, with the favourite failing to get around, a few of the other more-fancied runners coming up short and a pair stepping up from handicaps filling the places, the winner essentially a class better after doing barely enough in front after cruising there, the first 3 all at the trip for the first time. **Abacadabras** picked up his second Grade 1 of the season, stepped up 4f in trip, not required to improve but essentially better than the result, needing his mind made up after he'd got to the front really smoothly but rather earlier than ideal, likely to be competitive at the highest level for the foreseeable future, another try against Honeysuckle at Punchestown by no means a foregone conclusion; held up, travelled strongly, smooth headway after 3 out, hit next, going well when blundered last, led soon after, ridden out. **Buzz** proved better than ever, up in grade and trip, seeing things out thoroughly; held up, took keen hold, headway before 3 out, ridden after, kept on well run-in; he ran in the Betfair Hurdle last time, the form of which has proved predictably very solid, despite neither first nor second giving their running next time out. **Millers Bank** in good form in handicaps, excelled himself, up in grade and trip, seeing the extra distance out well; in touch, travelled well, headway entering straight, shaken up after 3 out, kept on run-in; he's a really likeable type and there's no reason to doubt the improvement shown, despite his starting price. **Buveur d'Air** looked more his old self than he had at Haydock, despite being warm and a bit edgy beforehand, his earlier exertions costing him a place late on; handy, took keen hold, not fluent second, led eighth, hampered next, ridden after, headed soon after last, no extra final 100 yds; there would be limited options for him for the rest of the season. **Brewin'upastorm** wasn't in the same form as the last time or the time before, perhaps just being back in a more competitive environment the issue; held up, not fluent fourth, shaken up 3 out, made no impression; he's likely to continue to need to be carefully placed. **Silver Streak** ran respectably, reverted to more patient tactics, faring much better than he had in this race in 2019, though he was probably stretched by the trip, likely to benefit from a return to around 2m; waited with, headway entering straight, shaken up before 2 out, no extra last. **Not So Sleepy** ran respectably, a mix of stamina being stretched and not being up to the task over a 4f longer trip; prominent, left in front seventh, headed next, weakened after 3 out. **Mcfabulous** failed to meet expectations, his last 2 runs rather underwhelming after such a promising start to the campaign, though the Select Hurdle at Sandown might be just the race to give him a more positive end to the season; prominent, not fluent third, ridden before straight, weakened run-in. **Ballyandy** was well held, going with little zest; not always fluent, labouring sixth, always behind. **Jason The Militant** upped in trip, departed too far out to say what would have happened; led until unseated rider seventh. **Song For Someone** back up in trip, having been a late absentee from the Champion Hurdle, ran even worse than he had at Wincanton, sluggish at the start after being asked to jump off with the leaders and never looking comfortable at any stage, a real shame after such a fine season; dropped to near last jumping first, in mid-field after second, lost place again fifth, pulled up seventh.

AINTREE Friday April 9
GOOD to SOFT

Betway Mildmay Novices' Chase (Grade 1) (1)

Pos	Btn	Horse	Age	Wgt	Eq	Trainer	Jockey	SP
1		CHANTRY HOUSE (IRE)	7	11-4		Nicky Henderson	Nico de Boinville	11/8f
2	32	SHAN BLUE (IRE)	7	11-4		Dan Skelton	Harry Skelton	9/2
3	26	FIDDLERONTHEROOF (IRE)	7	11-4	(t)	Colin Tizzard	Robbie Power	15/2
F		ESPOIR DE ROMAY (FR)	7	11-4	(t)	Kim Bailey	David Bass	17/2
pu		EMPIRE STEEL (IRE)	7	11-4		Sandy Thomson	Ryan Mania	12/1
pu		SPORTING JOHN (IRE)	6	11-4		Philip Hobbs	Tom O'Brien	16/1
pu		THE BIG BREAKAWAY (IRE)	6	11-4		Colin Tizzard	Harry Cobden	5/1

7 ran Race Time 6m 29.90 Closing Sectional (3.15f): 53s (92.9%) Winning Owner: Mr John P. McManus

Favourite beats second favourite to confirm their form from Cheltenham might sound routine yet this was anything but a nothing-to-see-here Grade 1 novice, one which—thanks to a string of lacklustre efforts—had already been reduced to a slow-motion head-to-head by the time the pace-forcing Espoir de Romay stood off too far at the second last, leaving Chantry House to labour his way to his festival double. **Chantry House** is a very smart novice but one who's had the rub of the green in landing back-to-back festival Grade 1 events, seeing Envoi Allen's early fall open the door in the Marsh and Espoir de Romay's much later one here handing him this, probably not all out at the time but still more than 2 lengths behind a winner who'd had plenty of opportunity to give way before then as Chantry House had tried to close the gap from 4 out, looking tired as he got over the last yet clearly in no danger by then; he's failed to fire only once in his Rules career but will have to raise his game to be a major player at the top level in open company. **Shan Blue** gives the impression he'll be best short of staying trips but a 3-week rest following his race-breaking effort in the Marsh (when much closer to Chantry House) might well have been a factor in his tame finishing effort as well, either way sure to be better judged on some of the positive work he's done in his first season chasing when he returns next time around; he pressed the leader and jumped fine bar hitting the twelfth, but he began to crack once shaken up after 4 out and went to nothing in the straight, left to claim a hollow second when Espoir de Romay fell 2 out. **Fiddlerontheroof** was almost certainly still feeling the effects of his unequal battle with Monkfish, out again only 3 weeks on and making it clear early on he wasn't on song, much like his stablemate who didn't even complete; raced off the pace, jumped sketchily, never going well from fourth, struggling some way out. **Espoir de Romay** came without the Cheltenham baggage that seemed to ail a few of the others and still hadn't been pegged back by Chantry House when launching himself at the second last and crumpling on landing, set to raise his game another notch up to this level whether he'd have held on or not, rated for now as having won by a length rather than the 2½ lengths he was ahead at the time; his jumping under a positive ride had been a big asset prior to his mishap, and he's got the attributes to do well back in leading handicaps next season, with so many to go at from 2½m and beyond. **Empire Steel** is best excused this run, asked a totally contrasting question to those he's answered before (hiked in grade on far less testing going) and finding it a shock to the system 7 weeks on from his defeat of an off-colour Protektorat in the Kelso mud; in touch, lost place when hit eighth, began to lose touch twelfth but very much looked after and eventually pulled up 5 out. **Sporting John** has gone from a promising staying novice prospect to one seemingly bereft of confidence, never jumping/travelling with any purpose in rear (worst mistake second) even before his new rider called it a day at the ninth; perhaps a return to testing ground following a break will see him revive in the autumn. **The Big Breakaway** ran no sort of race, having been out on his feet at the end of the Broadway just 3 weeks prior, his (and his stablemate's effort) peculiarly perhaps more a boost than a knock to Monkfish, who'd forced both into enduring gruelling races then; in touch early, lost place before halfway, blundered eleventh, lost touch back straight.

Marsh Chase (Melling) (Grade 1) (1)

Pos	Btn	Horse	Age	Wgt	Eq	Trainer	Jockey	SP
1		FAKIR D'OUDAIRIES (FR)	6	11-7		Joseph Patrick O'Brien, Ireland	M. P. Walsh	2/1f
2	11	NUTS WELL	10	11-7		Ann Hamilton	Danny McMenamin	14/1
3	1¼	ITCHY FEET (FR)	7	11-7		Olly Murphy	Gavin Sheehan	14/1
4	13	POLITOLOGUE (FR)	10	11-7	(t)	Paul Nicholls	Harry Cobden	5/2
5	2	DUC DES GENIEVRES (FR)	8	11-7	(h+t)	Paul Nicholls	Lorcan Williams	40/1
6	4	MASTER TOMMYTUCKER	10	11-7		Paul Nicholls	Sam Twiston-Davies	13/2
7	5	NOTEBOOK (GER)	8	11-7	(t)	Henry de Bromhead, Ireland	Rachael Blackmore	9/2

7 ran   Race Time 5m 04.00   Closing Sectional (3.15f): 48.5s (99.2%)   Winning Owner: Mr John P. McManus

One of those Aintree showpiece events that didn't suffer from any sort of Cheltenham hangover, given more than half the field eschewed last month all together and one of those that did turn out again proved a class apart to hand the Irish yet another Grade 1 on these shores this spring; Master Tommytucker ensured a true gallop for all he wasn't taken on, yet it still got messy in the straight as the others fought for position in the winner's wake. **Fakir d'Oudairies** has ended his season on a high and probably delivered another personal best as he went one better than in the Ryanair for all this was clearly a lesser Grade 1, finally getting off the mark for the season and paying some compliment to the unrelenting powerhouse Allaho, whose position as Timeform's highest-rated jumper in training can only have been strengthened in the aftermath; close up early before settling into a clear third, he largely jumped very quickly and settled matters in little time once asked after being held together initially on bursting to the front soon after 3 out, clearly firmly at home under these sort of conditions despite a wealth of form on soft/heavy; if it wasn't certain at the start of the season, it's obvious now that 2½m is his optimum trip, and it's possible the door in the division will be opened more clearly next season if Allaho was to take a Champion Chase route instead. **Nuts Well** picked up right where he'd left off in the Old Roan (when seeing off improving Clondaw Castle as well as Itchy Feet), presumably saved for this since and returning from his break right on song once more, no match for the wide-margin winner but still showing he is indeed a credible force near the top level for all such a suggestion at the start of his yard's remarkable campaign would have been far fetched in the extreme; he might well have finished a clearer second, too, without trouble as the race was developing soon after 3 out, squeezed out and forced to switch as he was making his move but sticking at it even after hitting the second last. **Itchy Feet** benefited as expected from the drop back in trip after 7 weeks off, seeing things out better and, what's more, keeping mistakes to a minimum returned straight to chasing, narrowing the gap a little to Nuts Well from the Old Roan here; held up, he seemed to hang right in the back straight but was back on an even keel by the time he was shaken up after 3 out, sustaining his run into third crossing the last. **Politologue** had seen his Champion Chase defence ended before it had begun thanks to a bleed at the eleventh hour and, worryingly, the same issue manifested itself in the race itself here in his bid to regain his Melling crown, seeing him go from looking set to finish second as close to home as 2 out to wilting out of the placings; his days at the top level are probably numbered, especially with Shishkin, stablemate Hitman and possibly Allaho set to strengthen the division considerably next season. **Duc des Genievres** extended a losing run dating back to the 2019 Arkle, his season going to little since having his pocket picked by Put The Kettle On in a gruelling Shloer on his return; waited with, shaken up after 4 out, some headway 2 out, effort proved short-lived. **Master Tommytucker** is nothing if not a gripping watch, reverting to type with a roller-coaster display that showed he's anything but a reformed character, forcing the pace, stumbling on landing and very nearly unseating at the fourth, clouting the tenth and headed soon after another untidy leap 3 out, hanging left and folding then. **Notebook** continues to disappoint on these shores, ridden even more patiently and not responding at all when shaken up after 4 out.

Doom Bar Sefton Novices' Hurdle (Grade 1) (1)

Pos	Btn	Horse	Age	Wgt	Eq	Trainer	Jockey	SP
1		AHOY SENOR (IRE)	6	11-4		Lucinda Russell	Derek Fox	66/1
2	7	BRAVEMANSGAME (FR)	6	11-4		Paul Nicholls	Harry Cobden	13/8f
3	8	OSCAR ELITE (IRE)	6	11-4	(t)	Colin Tizzard	Jonjo O'Neill Jr.	15/2
4	6½	STREETS OF DOYEN (IRE)	7	11-4	(s+t)	John McConnell, Ireland	S. D. Torrens	11/2
5	3¼	DOYEN BREED (IRE)	6	11-4	(s)	Sandy Thomson	Ryan Mania	33/1
6	55	PATS FANCY (IRE)	6	11-4		Rebecca Curtis	Sean Bowen	80/1
F		MIDNIGHT RIVER	6	11-4		Dan Skelton	Harry Skelton	4/1
F		TOPOFTHECOTSWOLDS (IRE)	7	11-4		Nigel Twiston-Davies	Sam Twiston-Davies	50/1
pu		BOTHWELL BRIDGE (IRE)	6	11-4		Nicky Henderson	James Bowen	16/1
pu		CHAMPAGNESUPEROVER (IRE)	6	11-4	(t)	Olly Murphy	A. P. Heskin	28/1
pu		GALLYHILL (IRE)	6	11-4		Nicky Henderson	Nico de Boinville	11/2
pu		SIZABLE SAM	6	11-4		Jeremy Scott	Matt Griffiths	25/1

12 ran   Race Time 6m 14.40   Closing Sectional (3.15f): 47.5s (100.6%)   Winning Owner: Mrs C Wymer & Mr PJS Russell

A huge-priced winner but there was no apparent fluke about his all-the-way success, the pace having been sound and his 2 nearest pursuers lining up following placed efforts at the Cheltenham Festival. **Ahoy Senor** overcame the considerable rise in class upped further in trip in some style, evoking memories of his stable's other Grade 1 novice hurdle winner, the ill-fated Brindisi Breeze, with a tremendously likeable front-running performance, some effort to do this on just his second run over hurdles; made running, jumped fluently, went with enthusiasm, shaken up after last, driven clear; he'll reportedly go chasing next season and has all the hallmarks of a really smart novice if he stays sound and continues to go the right way. **Bravemansgame** had no problem with the longer trip and just seemed to bump into a better one on the day, no real sign that he hadn't recovered from Cheltenham; mid-field, close up 4 out, effort next, second last, kept on, no match for winner; he's had a fine season even if it's stalled a bit since the Challow and will surely raise his game over fences next season. **Oscar Elite** ran creditably as he made the places in another Grade 1 novice, this probably a match for what he did at Cheltenham; chased leader, pushed along after 3 out, mistake next, one paced; he's a smart novice chaser in the making for next season. **Streets of Doyen** ran respectably in first-time tongue strap, just lacking the gears to keep up; held up, outpaced 4 out, left in frame next, plugged on. **Doyen Breed** ran as well as entitled to, facing a much stiffer task stepping out of fairly useful Scottish handicaps; held up, outpaced 4 out, plugged on; he's the type his trainer will do well with over fences next season. **Pats Fancy** faced another stiff task; in touch, pushed along home turn, folded.

Midnight River looked to be in the process of running well when departing, though he went just as things were set to take shape and did have stamina to prove up half a mile in trip; patiently ridden, in touch when fell 3 out. **Topofthecotswolds** was off the pace when falling at the fifth. **Bothwell Bridge** was either not right or just found out in better company; mid-division, lost place before 4 out, soon beaten. **Champagnesuperover** ran badly, perhaps not right to perform so lamentably; in rear, struggling 4 out. **Gallyhill** ran better than being pulled up suggests but went out alarmingly quickly and was said to have made a respiratory noise; in touch, pushed along home turn, folded. **Sizable Sam** wasn't up to this better company; close up, mistake second, lost place 4 out, beaten when clouted 3 out; he should do well at the right level over fences next season.

AINTREE Saturday April 10
GOOD to SOFT

Doom Bar Maghull Novices' Chase (Grade 1) (1)

Pos	Btn	Horse	Age	Wgt	Eq	Trainer	Jockey	SP
1		SHISHKIN (IRE)	7	11-4		Nicky Henderson	Nico de Boinville	1/8f
2	3¼	FUNAMBULE SIVOLA (FR)	6	11-4		Venetia Williams	Charlie Deutsch	14/1
3	20	GUMBALL (FR)	7	11-4		Philip Hobbs	Tom O'Brien	16/1
4	24	LONGHOUSE SALE (IRE)	7	11-4	(t)	Dan Skelton	Harry Skelton	28/1
F		ELVIS MAIL (FR)	7	11-4		N. W. Alexander	Conor O'Farrell	18/1

5 ran Race Time 3m 56.10 Closing Sectional (3.15f): 45.5s (103.5%) Winning Owner: Mrs J Donnelly

Not quite the procession for Shishkin that the market anticipated, partly as a result of not being at his best, but also partly as a result of marked improvement from the runner-up, the pair finishing a long way clear in a truly-run race. **Shishkin** completed his task in not much better than workmanlike fashion, perhaps not fully over his exertions at Cheltenham, though that might underestimate the runner-up; tracked pace, travelled well, led approaching fifth, ridden 2 out, not fluent last, kept on run-in, always holding on. **Funambule Sivola** has made remarkable progress in handicaps this season and took his form up another notch, stepped into top novice company, briefly looking a threat to the winner and sticking to his task, even though unable to land a blow; in touch, travelled well, took second early in straight, shaken up after 2 out, kept on run-in; he's stood up well to a busy campaign, his task to sustain his form faced with what will be stiff assignments wherever he goes next season. **Gumball** was well held, back over fences, not good enough to lead the winner until even halfway; led until approaching fifth, chased leader after, mistake 3 out, weakened. **Longhouse Sale** was out of his depth, handicaps into the spring and summer likely to be more up his street; in touch, left behind after 4 out. **Elvis Mail** faced a stiff task in this grade and would have finished around where the third did had he not fallen, his jumping not quite up to the demands of these fences; in rear, not fluent second, seventh, shaken up straight, fourth when fell 2 out.

TIMEFORM'S BEST OF 2020/21

When Minella Times won the Grand National at Aintree, he crowned an unparalleled season of big-race success for trainer Henry de Bromhead and jockey Rachael Blackmore. Blackmore became the first female rider to win the National three weeks on from her record-breaking achievements at the Cheltenham Festival, a meeting at which she was crowned the leading jockey with six winners in total. Four of those winners, including the brilliant Honeysuckle in the Champion Hurdle, were trained by De Bromhead, who also won the Champion Chase with Put The Kettle On and the Gold Cup with Minella Indo, the latter beating the Blackmore-ridden A Plus Tard in a one-two for the stable. No other trainer in history has won the Champion Hurdle, Champion Chase and Gold Cup in the same season and, for good measure, De Bromhead also saddled a one-two in the Grand National as Balko des Flos filled the runner-up spot behind Minella Times. Honeysuckle went on to extend her winning sequence under Rules to 12 with victory in the Punchestown Champion Hurdle on her final start, but even the best efforts of De Bromhead weren't enough to end the dominance of Willie Mullins on home soil. Indeed, Mullins had wrapped up his fifteenth Irish trainers' championship long before the season-ending Punchestown Festival, where he signed off in style with a remarkable haul of 19 winners. They included Chacun Pour Soi, who once again ended the season as Timeform's highest-rated jumps horse in training after a stunning success in the Punchestown Champion Chase. Mullins also edged out De Bromhead on countback to be crowned the leading trainer at the Cheltenham Festival, a meeting at which Irish trainers saddled 23 of the 28 winners. Paul Nicholls drew a blank at Cheltenham for the first time since 2002, but wins for the likes of Politologue in the Tingle Creek Chase and Frodon in the King George VI Chase ensured that Nicholls still won the British trainers' championship for the twelfth time in his career. Politologue was ridden to victory at Sandown by Harry Skelton, one of five Grade 1 winners during the latest season for the newly crowned champion jockey.

Staying chasers

Much of the attention heading into the 2021 edition of the Cheltenham Gold Cup centred around **Al Boum Photo** (c170), who was attempting to become the first three-time winner of the race since Best Mate completed his famous hat-trick in 2004. Al Boum Photo followed a tried-and-tested path to the Festival, blowing the cobwebs away with a straightforward victory in a Grade 3 at Tramore on New Year's Day, and he was sent off the 9/4 favourite to win the Gold Cup, with the Savills Chase winner **A Plus Tard** (c174) and the first two from the previous year's RSA Chase, **Champ** (c167+) and **Minella Indo** (c175), heading the list of dangers. Minella Indo had featured amongst the ante-post favourites after returning with a pair of routine wins in lesser company at Wexford and Navan, but his Gold Cup prospects had taken a knock in a couple of subsequent starts at Leopardstown as he fell in the Savills Chase before finishing only fourth behind **Kemboy** (c166) in the Irish Gold Cup. Rachael Blackmore had the difficult task of choosing between stablemates A Plus Tard and Minella Indo in the Gold Cup, but the race itself would have made easy viewing

Minella Indo leads A Plus Tard over the final fence in the Gold Cup

for trainer Henry de Bromhead as his two runners gradually moved clear of Al Boum Photo in the straight. Minella Indo, with Jack Kennedy deputising in the saddle after Blackmore sided with A Plus Tard, was always just getting the better of the argument and kept finding all the way to the line to land the spoils by a length and a quarter, with another four and a quarter lengths back to Al Boum Photo in third. Minella Indo ranks as one of the best Gold Cup winners in the last decade and, still only an eight-year-old, he should continue to take plenty of beating in this division in 2021/22. Incidentally, the Punchestown Gold Cup had been on the agenda for Minella Indo after Cheltenham, but a bruised foot on the eve of the race brought his campaign to a premature end. That left Al Boum Photo to represent the Gold Cup form at Punchestown but, in the event, it was a horse who missed Cheltenham altogether who came out on top in the shape of **Clan des Obeaux** (c170), who had also won the Bowl Chase at Aintree by 26 lengths since finishing only third in his bid to win the King George VI Chase for the third year in succession. Paul Nicholls was still celebrating at Kempton, though, as **Frodon** (c166) made all under an excellent ride from Bryony Frost to provide the yard with a record twelfth win in the Boxing Day highlight, jumping superbly and digging deep under pressure to beat **Waiting Patiently** (c163) by two and a quarter lengths. **Cyrname** (c166§), another stablemate of Frodon, went off the boil after showing top-class form to win the Charlie Hall Chase at Wetherby on his reappearance, blowing out completely in both the King George and Ascot Chase. Other

Grade 1 winners in this division earlier in the season included **The Storyteller** (c164), who won the Champion Chase at Down Royal, and **Bristol de Mai** (c166), who recorded his third success in the Betfair Chase at Haydock before chasing home **Native River** (c163) in the rearranged Cotswold Chase at Sandown. Native River and Frodon went on to fare best of the British team in the Gold Cup at Cheltenham, finishing fourth and fifth respectively behind Minella Indo.

Two-mile chasers

Chacun Pour Soi (c179) fluffed his lines when sent off the 13/8-on favourite for the Queen Mother Champion Chase at the Cheltenham Festival, but he was imperious on his other four starts during the latest season, culminating with a dazzling victory in the Punchestown Champion Chase. He was given a more attacking ride than usual on that occasion and quickly put the race to bed after the third last, just needing to be kept up to his work to beat stablemate **Allaho** (c176) by five and a half lengths. The timefigure provided plenty of substance to the form and Chacun Pour Soi's record since joining Willie Mullins—which now includes no less than five performances of 170 or above on Timeform ratings—marks him out as a 2m chaser out of the very top drawer. Allaho lacked the necessary pace to go with Chacun Pour Soi at Punchestown, but he proved himself a top-class chaser in his own right when putting up a breath-taking display to win the Ryanair Chase at Cheltenham. That was a wonderful exhibition of galloping and jumping from the front as he left several high-class rivals trailing in his wake, ultimately passing the post with 12 lengths to spare over **Fakir d'Oudairies** (c166), who ran out an 11-length winner of the Melling Chase at Aintree on his next start. The likes of **Min** (c171) and **Mister Fisher** (c166) were beaten out of sight in the Ryanair and, on this form, Allaho should be a major player in all the big races at around 2½m in 2021/22. The Champion Chase at Cheltenham went the way of the mare **Put The Kettle On** (c158), who showed an excellent attitude to get the verdict by half a length from **Nube Negra** (c165+), in the process becoming the first of her sex to ever win the race. It was a rather unsatisfactory contest overall, though, the gallop not as strong as expected and the field still very well grouped when there was major trouble on the inside after the third last. **Sceau Royal** (c163), who won the Game Spirit Chase at Newbury on his previous start, was nearly brought down in the melee and did very well under the circumstances to be beaten less than four lengths into fifth. There were also a couple of notable absentees at Cheltenham in the shape of dual winner **Altior** (c166), who was once again ruled out of the race a couple of days beforehand, and the 2020 winner **Politologue** (c164), a last-minute withdrawal after he was found to have blood in a nostril on saddling. Altior showed that he retains a lot of his old ability in two starts during the latest season, filling the runner-up spot in both the Desert Orchid Chase at Kempton (beaten three and a half lengths behind Nube Negra) and the Celebration Chase at Sandown (beaten three and three quarter lengths behind **Greaneteen** (c167)). Politologue beat stablemate Greaneteen when making a successful return in the Tingle Creek Chase at Sandown, but he failed to add to his tally in two subsequent starts in Grade 1 company, including when soundly put in his place by the enterprisingly-ridden **First Flow** (c163) in the Clarence House Chase at Ascot.

Novice chasers

Sadly, we were robbed of a clash between **Shishkin** (c171p) and **Energumene** (c169p) in the Sporting Life Arkle at the Cheltenham Festival due to the latter's injury, but that will hopefully be something to look forward to in 2021/22 after both horses went unbeaten through their novice campaigns. Shishkin produced the best performance in this division all season when successful at Cheltenham, having no Energumene to drive him on but still showing top-class form to win by 15 lengths. An outstanding chasing prospect, Shishkin is likely to dominate the open 2m division in Britain before taking on the best of the Irish at the major spring festivals in 2021/22. Energumene recovered from the setback which ruled him out of Cheltenham in time for Punchestown, where he didn't need to come off the bridle to beat his Grade 1-winning stablemate **Janidil** (c156) by 16 lengths in the Ryanair Novice Chase. The best is yet to come from Energumene and a Champion Chase featuring Chacun Pour Soi, Shishkin and him will be something to savour. **Monkfish** (c167p), who won the Broadway Novices' Chase at Cheltenham, was the dominant force in the staying ranks, putting up his best effort when beating **Latest Exhibition** (c155) by 11 lengths in the Flogas Novice Chase at Leopardstown. He had plausible excuses when losing his unbeaten record over fences in the Champion Novice Chase at Punchestown, making a terrible error just when he was being asked to

Shishkin romps to victory in the Sporting Life Arkle

close down the leader. It's still relatively early days in his chasing career and Monkfish will be well worth another chance to improve on the form of his impressive Flogas win (backed up by the timefigure) in 2021/22. The Champion Novice Chase was billed as a head-to-head between Monkfish and **Envoi Allen** (c160+), who was unbeaten in 11 starts under Rules before falling in the JLT Novices' Chase won by **Chantry House** (c156) at Cheltenham. In the event, however, **Colreevy** (c158) emerged from the pack to upset the pair of them on her final outing before retirement, making all to win by eight lengths from Monkfish, with Envoi Allen reportedly returning lame after he was pulled up before two out. Colreevy went to the paddocks with a perfect record over fences, with the inaugural renewal of the Mares' Chase at the Cheltenham Festival featuring amongst her other wins. **Galvin** (c158p) came out on top in a classy edition of the National Hunt Chase at Cheltenham, while Chantry House looks another promising young stayer having followed up his JLT success when stepped up to 3m in the Mildmay Novices' Chase at Aintree. The official winning margin was 32 lengths on the last occasion, though that doesn't tell the whole story as the result was still very much in the balance when **Espoir de Romay** (c155) took a crashing fall two out. The Dan Skelton yard was blessed in this department with **Allmankind** (c159), **Protektorat** (c154) and **Shan Blue** (c150+) all winning in Grade 1 company, while Venetia Williams tried her luck in the Gold Cup with **Royale Pagaille** (c163) after he showed high-class form to easily defy a BHA mark of 156 in the Peter Marsh Chase at Haydock. **Asterion Forlonge** (c162) also produced a big performance in handicap company when winning at the Punchestown Festival, finally delivering on his earlier promise as he conceded plenty of weight all round to his rivals.

Staying hurdlers

Flooring Porter (h164) was beaten in a handicap from a mark of 131 last October, which makes his rise to being crowned the Stayers' Hurdle winner at the Cheltenham Festival even more remarkable. He announced his arrival on the big stage when winning the Christmas Hurdle at Leopardstown, beating the best around in Ireland by six lengths, and his Cheltenham victory represented another step up the ladder as he once again made all to land the spoils by three and a quarter lengths from **Sire du Berlais** (h161). Flooring Porter wasn't in the same form on his final start at Punchestown, but his ability to sustain a strong gallop when on-song marks him out as a high-class staying hurdler. He has plenty of time on his side as a six-year-old, too, even if his running style isn't exactly reminiscent of those who have dominated this division this century. **Beacon Edge** (h160) shaped better than the bare result when fourth in the Stayers' Hurdle, looking the biggest threat to the winner for a long way before tiring late on. He then went to Punchestown for the Champion Stayers Hurdle and probably would have been placed but for falling two out, still to be asked for his effort at the time. **Klassical Dream** (h160) took advantage of Flooring Porter's below-par showing and Beacon Edge's fall to win the Champion Stayers Hurdle, proving well suited by the step up to 3m on his first start for 16 months. He travelled strongly in mid-division and quickly asserted after being produced to lead early in the straight, ultimately winning by nine lengths from stablemate **James du Berlais** (h152). Providing all remains well with him, Klassical Dream will now have the choice of going down the novice chasing route or remaining over timber, the latter option perhaps the more likely given that he's already sharing favouritism with **Thyme Hill** (h158) for the 2022 Stayers' Hurdle. Thyme Hill was forced to miss the latest renewal of that race due to a minor setback, but he still enjoyed a productive campaign, winning the Long Distance Hurdle at Newbury and Liverpool Hurdle at Aintree either side of a thrilling battle with **Paisley Park** (h159) in the Long Walk Hurdle at Ascot. Paisley Park came out on top by a neck on that occasion but couldn't add to his tally in two subsequent starts in Grade 1 company, finishing third in the Stayers' Hurdle before being pulled up in the Liverpool Hurdle. **McFabulous** (h155) and **Roksana** (h150) featured amongst the other standout performers in this division in Britain. McFabulous proved too good for **On The Blind Side** (h151) and **Thomas Darby** (h153) when winning the rearranged Relkeel Hurdle at Kempton, while Roksana produced her best effort when pushing Thyme Hill all the way to the line in the Liverpool Hurdle, ultimately losing out by a neck. She also finished a good third behind **Black Tears** (h152) and **Concertista** (h151) in the Mares' Hurdle at Cheltenham. Concertista went on to Punchestown where she finished third behind stablemate **Stormy Ireland** (h147)—back with the Willie Mullins yard after a disappointing spell with Paul Nicholls—in the Mares Champion Hurdle.

Two-mile hurdlers

Honeysuckle (h165) won all four starts during the latest season to maintain her perfect record under Rules, cementing her status as the best hurdler around. She kicked off with victories in the Hatton's Grace Hurdle at Fairyhouse and Irish Champion Hurdle at Leopardstown—both for the second year in a row—before running out an impressive winner of the biggest prize of them all in this division, the Champion Hurdle at the Cheltenham Festival. A couple of her chief market rivals weren't at their best, but Honeysuckle still showed top-class form to beat **Sharjah** (h164) by six and a half lengths, with the previous year's winner **Epatante** (h154) another three lengths back in third. That trio went on to fill the same three positions in the Punchestown Champion Hurdle and, though Sharjah more than halved the deficit, there was still no doubting Honeysuckle's overwhelming superiority. A real credit to her connections, she is now a nine-time Grade 1 winner and seems sure to add to that remarkable tally if continuing in the same sort of form in 2021/22. Sharjah had previously won the Matheson Hurdle at Leopardstown for the third consecutive year, just needing to be pushed out to beat **Aspire Tower** (h155) by two lengths, while Epatante ran out an effortless winner of the Fighting Fifth Hurdle at Newcastle before going off the boil, her collapse starting with a surprise defeat at the hands of **Silver Streak** (h154) in the Christmas Hurdle at Kempton. Goshen (h159) produced the best performance by a British-trained hurdler during the latest season when winning the Kingwell Hurdle at Wincanton by 22 lengths, but that effort now seems a distant memory given how poorly he ran at both Cheltenham and Punchestown. **Song For Someone** (h156), who won the Coral Hurdle at Ascot and International Hurdle at Cheltenham, was also on the fringes of the Champion Hurdle picture, but he ended up missing the Festival and signed off with a laboured effort when pulled up in the Aintree Hurdle won by **Abacadabras** (h159). An early faller in the Champion Hurdle, Abacadabras was value for extra at Aintree as he idled in front after making his effort earlier than ideal, ultimately getting the verdict by a length and a quarter from **Buzz** (h156). That was his second Grade 1 success of the season after also winning the Morgiana Hurdle at Punchestown, by a neck and

Honeysuckle is now unbeaten in 12 starts under Rules

a short head from **Saint Roi** (h154) and **Jason The Militant** (h157), and he had valid excuses when managing only fourth in the Punchestown Champion Hurdle on his final start (possibly found the race coming too soon). **Buveur d'Air** (h155) was back in fourth at Aintree, making just his second appearance after more than a year on the sidelines, while **Petit Mouchoir** (h157), who finished third behind Buveur d'Air in the 2017 Champion Hurdle, showed that he also retains plenty of ability when second from a BHA mark of 155 in the County Hurdle at Cheltenham. More recently, **Saldier** (h161) produced another notable performance in handicap company, showing high-class form to defy top weight in the Galway Hurdle in July. A dual Grade 1 winner earlier in his career, he beat a mix of unexposed sorts and seasoned handicappers at Galway in the style of one still capable of mixing it at a higher level.

Novice hurdlers

It was a close-run thing in this division between a pair of Cheltenham Festival winners, headlined by **Appreciate It** (h160p), who produced marginally the best effort when routing the opposition by 24 lengths in the Supreme Novices' Hurdle. That was a performance right out of the top drawer and entitles Appreciate It to be spoken of in the same terms as Douvan and Altior, the best recent winners of the Supreme. He is every inch a chaser on looks and seems likely to try and emulate that pair by winning next season's Arkle, for which he is already a short-priced favourite. The Ballymore Novices' Hurdle produced a winner of similar merit in the shape of **Bob Olinger** (h159p), who was well on top at the finish after travelling strongly throughout. He was produced to lead on the bridle two out and then showed a decisive turn of foot to leave a pair of previous Grade 1 winners trailing in his wake, ultimately passing the post with seven and a half lengths to spare over **Gaillard du Mesnil** (h151) and **Bravemansgame** (h146). A rangy, good sort on looks, Bob Olinger has top-class chaser written all over him and rates a really thrilling prospect for the switch to fences in 2021/22. Willie Mullins dominated the Grade 1 novice hurdles at the Punchestown Festival, with Gaillard du Mesnil making the most of Bob Olinger's absence to resume winning ways in the 2½m Champion Novice Hurdle. Mullins also won the 2m Champion Novice Hurdle with the mare **Echoes In Rain** (h151p), who showed even better form when landing a Grade 2 at Fairyhouse three weeks earlier, and the Irish Daily Mirror Novice Hurdle with **Galopin des Champs** (h150p), who took the step up to 3m in his stride to follow up his victory in the Martin Pipe Conditional Jockeys' Handicap Hurdle at Cheltenham. Galopin des Champs won by 12 lengths at Punchestown and his beaten rivals included **Vanillier** (h147), himself a wide-margin winner of the Albert Bartlett Novices' Hurdle at Cheltenham. That meeting also witnessed notable wins for **Telmesomethinggirl** (h140) and **Belfast Banter** (h143), who won the Mares' Novices' Hurdle and County Hurdle respectively. Belfast Banter went on to Grade 1 success at Aintree in the Top Novices' Hurdle, though he needed to show only useful form to make the breakthrough at that level. **My Drogo** (h156p), on the other hand, produced a very smart performance in winning the Mersey Novices' Hurdle, his fourth success from as many starts over timber. He was the best novice hurdler in Britain during the latest season and looks an exciting prospect for chasing in 2021/22. Similar comments apply to **Ahoy Senor** (h150p), who was making just his second start over hurdles when winning the Sefton Novices' Hurdle at Aintree, putting up a likeable front-running display to beat Bravemansgame by seven lengths. The Grand National Festival also witnessed the best effort by a juvenile hurdler during the latest season as **Monmiral** (h151p) maintained his unbeaten record in the Anniversary 4-Y-O Juvenile Hurdle, easily beating **Adagio** (h142) by seven and a half lengths. Adagio had previously filled the runner-up spot in the Triumph Hurdle at Cheltenham won by **Quilixios** (h146), who later shaped as if amiss when down the field in the Champion Four Year Old Hurdle fought out by **Jeff Kidder** (h143), **Zanahiyr** (h143) and **Haut En Couleurs** (h142p) at Punchestown.

HORSES TO FOLLOW
2020/21 STATISTICS (Britain)

TRAINERS (1,2,3 earnings)	Horses	Indiv'l Wnrs	Races Won	Runs	% Strike Rate	Stakes £
1 Paul Nicholls	191	109	176	705	25.0	2,384,653
2 Dan Skelton	196	80	148	757	19.6	1,756,456
3 H. de Bromhead, Ireland	32	7	8	39	20.5	1,483,055
4 Nicky Henderson	180	74	103	545	18.9	1,427,092
5 Jonjo O'Neill	114	49	71	479	14.8	845,878
6 Fergal O'Brien	156	69	104	563	18.5	770,420
7 W. P. Mullins, Ireland	61	7	7	64	10.9	758,654
8 Alan King	116	35	54	405	13.3	720,376
9 Nigel Twiston-Davies	130	40	60	524	11.5	693,493
10 Venetia Williams	75	35	53	302	17.5	650,895

JOCKEYS (by winners)	1st	2nd	3rd	Unpl	Total Rides	% Strike Rate
1 Harry Skelton	152	116	88	326	682	22.3
2 Brian Hughes	142	145	140	463	890	16.0
3 Harry Cobden	123	94	74	291	582	21.1
4 Nico de Boinville	85	63	42	220	410	20.7
5 Sam Twiston-Davies	83	95	90	369	637	13.0
6 Paddy Brennan	82	76	61	227	446	18.4
7 Richard Johnson	73	66	86	296	521	14.0
8 Sean Bowen	68	42	40	260	410	16.6
9 David Bass	66	36	33	212	347	19.0
10 Tom Scudamore	65	48	46	271	430	15.1

SIRES OF WINNERS (1,2,3 earnings)	Races Won	Runs	% Strike Rate	Stakes £
1 Stowaway (by Slip Anchor)	71	575	12.3	1,158,497
2 Oscar (by Sadler's Wells)	54	496	10.9	1,116,016
3 Yeats (by Sadler's Wells)	91	670	13.6	1,078,898
4 Flemensfirth (by Alleged)	78	550	14.2	979,249
5 Midnight Legend (by Night Shift)	76	634	12.0	891,924
6 Getaway (by Monsun)	101	818	12.3	826,093
7 Kapgarde (by Garde Royale)	37	278	13.3	701,296
8 Kayf Tara (by Sadler's Wells)	51	483	10.6	680,437
9 Milan (by Sadler's Wells)	65	636	10.2	650,000
10 Beneficial (by Top Ville)	39	352	11.1	632,835

LEADING HORSES (1,2,3 earnings)	Races Won	Runs	Stakes £
1 Minella Times 7 b.g Oscar - Triptoshan	1	1	375,000
2 Minella Indo 7 b.g Beat Hollow - Carrigeen Lily	1	1	263,766
3 Put The Kettle On 6 b.f Stowaway - Name For Fame	2	3	208,590
4 Honeysuckle 6 b.f Sulamani - First Royal	1	1	189,911
5 Frodon 8 b.g Nickname - Miss Country	3	5	172,372
6 Shishkin 6 b.g Sholokhov - Labarynth	5	5	164,982
7 Fakir D'Oudairies 5 b.g Kapgarde - Niagaria Du Bois	1	2	162,377
8 Allaho 6 b.g No Risk At All - Idaho Falls	1	1	155,290
9 The Shunter 7 b.g Stowaway - Tornado Lady	3	4	154,803
10 Clan Des Obeaux 8 b.g Kapgarde - Nausicaa Des Obeaux	1	4	153,549

SECTION

5

THE TIMEFORM TOP 100

Hurdlers

165	Honeysuckle	151	Navajo Pass	144	Kildisart	164	Bachasson
164	Flooring Porter	151	On The Blind Side	144	Unowhatimeanharry	164	Politologue
164	Sharjah	151	Pic d'Orhy	144	Wilde About Oscar	164	The Storyteller
162	Aramon	151	The Bosses Oscar	143p	Shewearsitwell	163	First Flow
161	Sire du Berlais	151	Younevercall	143	Belfast Banter	163	Native River
160p	Appreciate It	150p	Ahoy Senor	143	Call Me Lyreen	163	Notebook
160	Beacon Edge	150p	Galopin des Champs	143	Ciel de Neige	163	Presenting Percy
160	Klassical Dream	150	Roksana	143	Coeur Sublime	163	Royale Pagaille
159p	Bob Olinger	149	The Shunter	143	Guard Your Dreams	163	Sceau Royal
159	Abacadabras	148p	Capodanno	143	Hometown Boy	163	Waiting Patiently
159	Goshen	148	Bacardys	143	Jeff Kidder	162	Melon
159	Paisley Park	148	Ch'tibello	143	Minella Drama	162	Tornado Flyer
158	Thyme Hill	148	Decor Irlandais	143	Ribble Valley	162	Vinndication
157	Jason The Militant	148	Diol Ker	143	Third Time Lucki	161+	Santini
157	Petit Mouchoir	148	Edwardstone	143	Voix du Reve	161	Any Second Now
156p	My Drogo	148	Milkwood	143	Zanahiyr	161	Imperial Aura
156	Buzz	148	Next Destination	142	Ballyadam	161	Kalashnikov
156	Song For Someone	148	Sams Profile	142	Imperial Alcazar	161	Secret Investor
155+	Buveur d'Air	148	Third Wind	142	Kalashnikov	161§	Samcro
155	Aspire Tower	147	Agrapart	142	Lil Rockerfeller	160+	Delta Work
155	Summerville Boy	147	Cayd Boy	142	Minella Melody	160+	Envoi Allen
155	The Storyteller	147	Diego du Charmil	142	Molly Ollys Wishes	160	Dashel Drasher
155	Mcfabulous	147	Heaven Help Us	142	Sixshooter	160	Easy Game
154	Call Me Lord	147	Main Fact			160x	Cilaos Emery
154	Epatante	147	Scaramanga			159	Allmankind
154	Fury Road	147	Sole Pretender	## Chasers		159	Castlebawn West
154	Saint Roi	147	Stormy Ireland			159	Clondow Castle
154	Sceau Royal	147	Unexpected Depth	179	Chacun Pour Soi	159	Cloth Cap
154	Silver Streak	147	Vanillier	176	Allaho	159	Yala Enki
153	Ballyandy	147	Whiskey Sour	175	Minella Indo	158p	Galvin
153	Millers Bank	146	Bapaume	174	A Plus Tard	158	Chris's Dream
153	Thomas Darby	146	Blue Lord	171p	Shishkin	158	Colreevy
152	Black Tears	146	Bravemansgame	171	Min	158	Magic Saint
152	Brewin'upastorm	146	Christopher Wood	170	Al Boum Photo	158	Nuts Well
152	James du Berlais	146	Drop The Anchor	170	Clan des Obeaux	158	Put The Kettle On
152	Lisnagar Oscar	146	J'ai Froid	169p	Energumene	158	Rouge Vif
152	Not So Sleepy	146	Quilixios	167p	Monkfish	157+	Saint Calvados
152	Ronald Pump	145+	Bachasson	167	Champ	157	Dolos
151p	Echoes In Rain	145+	Bear Ghylls	167	Greaneteen	157	Pistol Whipped
151p	Monmiral	145	Ask Dillon	166	Altior	157	Sky Pirate
151+	Vinndication	145	Dandy Mag	166	Bristol de Mai	157x	Master Tommytucker
151	Concertista	145	Grand Roi	166	Fakir d'Oudairies	157d	Duc des Genievres
151	French Dynamite	145	Honest Vic	166	Frodon	156p	Ibleo
151	Gaillard du Mesnil	145	Indefatigable	166	Kemboy	156	Acapella Bourgeois
		145	Master McShee	166	Mister Fisher	156	Balko des Flos
		144	Friend Or Foe	166§	Cyrname	156	Bennys King
				165+	Nube Negra		

156	Cepage
156	Chantry House
156	Janidil
156	Lake View Lad
155p	Happygolucky
155+	Monalee
155	Castlegrace Paddy
155	Elimay
155	Espoir de Romay
155	Fusil Raffles
155	Latest Exhibition
155	Minella Times
155	Peregrine Run
155	Top Notch
154+	Tiger Roll
154	Aso
154	Daly Tiger
154	Funambule Sivola
154	Itchy Feet
154	Next Destination
154	Protektorat
154	Real Steel
154	Tout Est Permis
154§	Mister Malarky
153p	Escaria Ten
153+	Easysland
153	Al Dancer
153	Aye Right
153	Captain Guinness
153	Chatham Street Lad
153	Snow Falcon
152p	Hitman
152	Franco de Port
152	Sizing Pottsie

Juvenile Hurdlers

151p	Monmiral
146	Quilixios
143	Jeff Kidder
143	Zanahiyr
142p	Haut En Couleurs
142	Adagio
141	Tritonic
140p	Duffle Coat
139	Saint Sam
138p	French Aseel
138p	Stepney Causeway
137	Zoffanien
136	Teahupoo

135	Cabot Cliffs
133	Nassalam
131p	Good Ball
130	Fiveandtwenty
130	Historic Heart
129	Busselton
129	Druid's Altar
129	Ha d'Or
128+	Riviere d'Etel
128	Youmdor
127	Houx Gris
126	Her Indoors
126	Herbiers
126	Paros
125p	Goodbye Stranger
125p	Hystery Bere
125+	Coltor
125	Balko Saint
125	Casa Loupi
125	Hudson de Grugy
124p	Samarrive
124	Elham Valley
124	Homme Public
124	Sage Advice
124	Tinnahalla

Novice Hurdlers

160p	Appreciate It
159p	Bob Olinger
156p	My Drogo
151p	Echoes In Rain
151	Gaillard du Mesnil
150p	Ahoy Senor
150p	Galopin des Champs
149	The Shunter
148p	Capodanno
147	Vanillier
146	Blue Lord
146	Bravemansgame
145+	Bear Ghylls
145	Master McShee
144	Wilde About Oscar
143p	Shewearsitwell
143	Belfast Banter
143	Call Me Lyreen
143	Ciel de Neige
143	Guard Your Dreams
143	Minella Drama
143	Third Time Lucki

142	Ballyadam
142	Soaring Glory
141p	Flash Collonges
141	Ashdale Bob
141	Cape Gentleman
141	Crosshill
141	Colonel Mustard
141	For Pleasure
141	Jacksons Gold
140p	Pay The Piper
140	Calico
140	Faivoir
140	Metier
140	Shanroe
140	Telmesomethinggirl

Novice Chasers

171p	Shishkin
169p	Energumene
167p	Monkfish
163	Royale Pagaille
162	Asterion Forlonge
160+	Envoi Allen
159	Allmankind
158p	Galvin
158	Colreevy
157	Sky Pirate
156	Chantry House
156	Janidil
155p	Eklat de Rire
155p	Happygolucky
155	Espoir de Romay
155	Fusil Raffles
155	Latest Exhibition
154	Next Destination
154	Protektorat
153p	Escaria Ten
153	Captain Guinness
153	Chatham Street Lad
152p	Hitman
152	Franco de Port
151p	Pencilfulloflead
151	Andy Dufresne
151	Off You Go
150+	Shan Blue
150	Sporting John
150	The Shunter

National Hunt Flat Horses

124	Kilcruit
123	Sir Gerhard
118	O'Toole
117	Knappers Hill
116	Dysart Dynamo
116	Good Risk At All
116	Peking Rose
115	Stage Star
114+	Balco Coastal
114	Gerri Colombe
114	Letsbeclearaboutit
112	Grangee
111	Three Stripe Life
110p	Hollow Games
110p	Kilbeg King
110	Eileendover
110	Go Dante
109p	Shallwehaveonemore
109	Eric Bloodaxe
109	Harry Alonzo
109	Kyntara
109	Wonderwall
108p	Jonbon
108	Brooklynn Glory
108	Ginto
108	I Am Maximus
108	Me Too Pleae
108	Weseekhimhere
107	Gordon Dai Dai
106p	Grand Jury
106	Brandy Love
106	Elle Est Belle
106	Highland Charge
106	I Like To Move It
106	Luttrell Lad
106	Party Central
106	Rainyday Woman
106	Ramilles

TRAINERS FOR COURSES

The following statistics show the most successful trainers over the past five seasons at each of the courses that stage National Hunt racing in England, Scotland and Wales. Impact Value is expressed as a factor of a trainer's number of winners compared to those expected to occur by chance. Market Value is expressed as the factor by which the % chance of an Industry Starting Price exceeds random, as implied by field size. For example, a horse that is shorter than 3/1 in a 4-runner field will have a Market Value above 1.

AINTREE

Trainer	Wins	Runs	Strike Rate	% Rivals Beaten	P/L	Run To Form %	Impact Value	Market Value
Nicky Henderson	20	123	16.26%	53.20	-51.95	58.94	1.61	1.84
Dan Skelton	20	136	14.71%	59.62	39.60	68.38	1.28	1.54
Paul Nicholls	15	122	12.30%	52.69	-41.09	53.69	1.27	1.72
Colin Tizzard	11	79	13.92%	54.15	60.33	55.06	1.44	1.33
Tom George	9	73	12.33%	53.76	-2.67	50.00	1.33	1.25
Nigel Twiston-Davies	8	92	8.70%	50.17	-53.00	51.63	0.96	1.48
Alan King	8	53	15.09%	58.49	-7.88	66.98	1.70	1.59
Harry Fry	8	42	19.05%	58.25	6.73	63.10	1.71	1.40
Jonjo O'Neill	6	58	10.34%	43.24	-29.58	44.83	1.10	1.41
David Pipe	5	51	9.80%	53.57	-11.38	50.00	1.15	1.33

ASCOT

Trainer	Wins	Runs	Strike Rate	% Rivals Beaten	P/L	Run To Form %	Impact Value	Market Value
Nicky Henderson	35	164	21.34%	61.25	8.85	73.17	1.65	1.87
Paul Nicholls	30	190	15.79%	53.45	-19.63	61.84	1.18	1.54
Dan Skelton	11	77	14.29%	48.64	9.53	52.60	1.22	0.98
Harry Fry	10	56	17.86%	55.14	-13.50	62.50	1.66	1.60
Nigel Twiston-Davies	9	73	12.33%	48.05	-11.75	55.48	1.06	1.21
Dr Richard Newland	8	39	20.51%	60.30	24.25	66.67	1.74	1.22
Colin Tizzard	8	81	9.88%	49.77	-26.96	56.17	0.78	1.01
Gary Moore	8	96	8.33%	42.78	-50.80	40.63	0.74	0.99
Philip Hobbs	7	80	8.75%	52.13	-40.07	60.63	0.73	1.28
David Pipe	7	35	20.00%	59.70	19.00	60.00	2.08	1.05

AYR

Trainer	Wins	Runs	Strike Rate	% Rivals Beaten	P/L	Run To Form %	Impact Value	Market Value
Nicky Richards	39	188	20.74%	60.22	-37.00	61.97	1.65	1.85
Lucinda Russell	27	239	11.30%	52.86	-46.12	55.02	0.89	1.03
N. W. Alexander	27	218	12.39%	53.61	-15.17	55.28	1.02	1.00
Sandy Thomson	16	95	16.84%	56.91	-30.45	60.00	1.34	1.59
Donald McCain	13	67	19.40%	47.47	-22.31	52.24	1.35	1.38
Iain Jardine	13	83	15.66%	53.69	-15.32	51.81	1.33	1.12
Ian Duncan	13	118	11.02%	50.58	-28.75	51.27	0.90	0.78
Dan Skelton	12	52	23.08%	70.71	-5.87	73.08	2.03	1.88
Stuart Crawford, Ireland	10	86	11.63%	49.14	-27.75	55.81	0.95	1.25
Gordon Elliott, Ireland	10	51	19.61%	64.44	-20.37	69.61	1.48	2.20

BANGOR-ON-DEE

Trainer	Wins	Runs	Strike Rate	% Rivals Beaten	P/L	Run To Form %	Impact Value	Market Value
Donald McCain	65	308	21.10%	61.01	62.25	62.01	1.62	1.38
Dan Skelton	28	131	21.37%	56.81	-30.40	57.63	1.72	1.93
Alan King	18	65	27.69%	68.91	-4.29	70.00	1.98	2.37
Nigel Twiston-Davies	15	79	18.99%	58.97	-12.43	58.23	1.46	1.68
Jonjo O'Neill	13	82	15.85%	51.10	-10.83	54.88	1.34	1.22
Jennie Candlish	12	76	15.79%	55.72	-15.08	52.63	1.36	1.17
Henry Daly	12	49	24.49%	60.16	43.75	59.18	2.04	1.12
Fergal O'Brien	10	43	23.26%	61.03	5.60	56.98	1.80	1.59
Kim Bailey	8	46	17.39%	54.18	-20.24	60.87	1.50	1.53
Nicky Henderson	8	47	17.02%	58.96	-26.14	59.57	1.28	2.27

CARLISLE

Trainer	Wins	Runs	Strike Rate	% Rivals Beaten	P/L	Run To Form %	Impact Value	Market Value
Donald McCain	24	193	12.44%	57.04	-55.97	60.88	0.97	1.35
Nicky Richards	24	98	24.49%	58.14	35.29	60.20	1.80	1.45
Sue Smith	13	119	10.92%	48.58	-45.55	50.42	0.86	1.14
Stuart Crawford, Ireland	12	44	27.27%	67.06	4.54	71.59	2.04	1.57
Rose Dobbin	12	71	16.90%	48.70	-5.42	56.34	1.40	1.17
Micky Hammond	11	117	9.40%	40.72	-12.23	38.46	0.76	0.75
Brian Ellison	11	65	16.92%	55.97	-5.41	58.46	1.48	1.47
Lucinda Russell	11	137	8.03%	46.69	-10.25	43.80	0.70	0.96
Sandy Thomson	9	53	16.98%	48.05	-0.01	53.77	1.26	1.44
Nigel Twiston-Davies	9	34	26.47%	62.21	0.92	69.12	2.01	2.48

TRAINERS FOR COURSES

CARTMEL

Trainer	Wins	Runs	Strike Rate	% Rivals Beaten	P/L	Run To Form %	Impact Value	Market Value
Donald McCain	25	142	17.61%	61.15	-25.98	60.92	1.32	1.47
Peter Bowen	21	88	23.86%	56.39	32.34	56.25	1.81	1.63
James Moffatt	21	212	9.91%	48.99	-24.72	44.58	0.80	1.09
Dianne Sayer	11	81	13.58%	47.58	-36.50	40.12	1.18	1.18
Martin Todhunter	10	47	21.28%	60.84	-1.13	56.38	1.77	1.54
Sam England	8	33	24.24%	56.70	45.75	54.55	2.25	1.19
Ben Haslam	6	18	33.33%	64.12	106.50	61.11	2.83	1.05
Neil Mulholland	6	32	18.75%	43.63	-11.55	46.88	1.15	1.45
Micky Hammond	6	100	6.00%	48.30	-74.38	44.00	0.51	1.07
Gordon Elliott, Ireland	5	18	27.78%	75.48	-1.38	86.11	2.31	2.36

CATTERICK BRIDGE

Trainer	Wins	Runs	Strike Rate	% Rivals Beaten	P/L	Run To Form %	Impact Value	Market Value
Donald McCain	21	140	15.00%	58.64	-22.98	61.79	1.22	1.56
Sue Smith	18	86	20.93%	58.08	-13.10	55.23	1.70	1.44
Micky Hammond	15	167	8.98%	47.15	-38.50	41.62	0.77	0.84
Rebecca Menzies	10	45	22.22%	60.16	34.21	57.78	1.94	1.15
Dan Skelton	9	45	20.00%	55.38	-21.22	64.44	1.54	2.60
Sam England	9	55	16.36%	56.53	-11.59	60.91	1.25	1.34
Philip Kirby	9	73	12.33%	50.73	6.21	50.00	1.17	0.82
Jamie Snowden	8	17	47.06%	76.83	1.98	76.47	2.97	1.97
Tim Easterby	6	49	12.24%	51.05	-0.75	47.96	1.18	0.81
Brian Ellison	6	30	20.00%	56.66	-12.21	55.00	1.56	1.67

CHELTENHAM

Trainer	Wins	Runs	Strike Rate	% Rivals Beaten	P/L	Run To Form %	Impact Value	Market Value
Nicky Henderson	51	345	14.78%	54.35	-67.54	61.16	1.61	1.75
W. P. Mullins, Ireland	31	283	10.95%	55.68	-0.78	67.14	1.57	1.82
Gordon Elliott, Ireland	30	186	16.13%	61.00	67.55	66.40	2.42	2.01
Paul Nicholls	26	289	9.00%	51.49	-121.57	58.48	0.92	1.44
Colin Tizzard	26	253	10.28%	48.35	-84.63	55.53	1.03	1.11
Nigel Twiston-Davies	21	251	8.37%	50.29	-107.18	55.18	0.86	1.20
Dan Skelton	19	230	8.26%	53.39	-81.49	60.65	0.87	1.25
Fergal O'Brien	18	166	10.84%	54.83	-7.75	62.95	1.20	1.29
Henry de Bromhead, Ireland	17	115	14.78%	51.67	40.35	60.00	1.56	1.25
Philip Hobbs	12	181	6.63%	49.63	-129.13	54.14	0.73	1.36

CHEPSTOW

Trainer	Wins	Runs	Strike Rate	% Rivals Beaten	P/L	Run To Form %	Impact Value	Market Value
Paul Nicholls	49	181	27.07%	67.40	16.20	76.52	2.26	2.38
Evan Williams	30	228	13.16%	53.78	7.33	55.26	1.29	1.36
Philip Hobbs	28	151	18.54%	55.16	-8.95	57.28	1.77	1.75
Colin Tizzard	28	211	13.27%	55.57	-69.67	56.40	1.24	1.49
David Pipe	17	88	19.32%	64.27	16.98	61.93	1.93	1.53
Venetia Williams	16	115	13.91%	55.36	-45.89	57.83	1.30	1.41
Dan Skelton	14	108	12.96%	53.93	-0.43	52.78	1.23	1.40
Tom Lacey	13	49	26.53%	63.92	64.63	64.29	2.47	1.48
Tom George	12	82	14.63%	53.40	-31.62	55.49	1.41	1.43
Neil Mulholland	12	93	12.90%	50.01	-11.72	48.39	1.42	1.06

DONCASTER

Trainer	Wins	Runs	Strike Rate	% Rivals Beaten	P/L	Run To Form %	Impact Value	Market Value
Nicky Henderson	26	95	27.37%	63.65	-21.18	66.32	2.12	2.63
Paul Nicholls	18	72	25.00%	56.33	-10.16	65.28	1.59	1.69
Dan Skelton	17	98	17.35%	54.12	-28.55	56.63	1.32	1.45
Alan King	16	123	13.01%	57.06	-39.15	58.13	0.98	1.53
Ian Williams	14	80	17.50%	49.92	44.29	51.88	1.46	1.19
Ben Pauling	12	69	17.39%	47.39	55.63	44.93	1.47	1.16
Emma Lavelle	11	44	25.00%	63.42	3.07	62.50	2.14	1.66
Charlie Longsdon	11	88	12.50%	49.18	-6.55	57.95	1.08	1.06
Jonjo O'Neill	10	84	11.90%	54.42	-24.64	52.98	1.11	1.16
Ben Case	9	37	24.32%	63.05	48.21	62.16	2.07	0.96

EXETER

Trainer	Wins	Runs	Strike Rate	% Rivals Beaten	P/L	Run To Form %	Impact Value	Market Value
Paul Nicholls	35	117	29.91%	65.89	-12.08	70.94	2.19	2.40
Philip Hobbs	34	215	15.81%	56.52	-82.10	63.95	1.31	1.79
Colin Tizzard	33	202	16.34%	57.84	-73.56	60.15	1.41	1.59
Harry Fry	23	78	29.49%	66.13	25.51	70.51	2.61	2.73
David Pipe	18	180	10.00%	50.35	-78.48	50.00	0.99	1.44
Evan Williams	17	94	18.09%	47.85	21.63	50.00	1.38	1.24
Susan Gardner	15	116	12.93%	48.18	-17.13	43.53	1.17	0.89
Jeremy Scott	11	114	9.65%	56.67	-50.68	55.70	0.97	1.24
Venetia Williams	11	71	15.49%	54.17	-22.22	58.45	1.40	1.49
Emma Lavelle	10	59	16.95%	61.09	5.50	72.88	1.65	1.84

TRAINERS FOR COURSES

FAKENHAM

Trainer	Wins	Runs	Strike Rate	% Rivals Beaten	P/L	Run To Form %	Impact Value	Market Value
Olly Murphy	31	139	22.30%	58.65	-17.60	61.15	1.35	1.51
Lucy Wadham	19	65	29.23%	59.97	14.03	66.15	1.99	1.46
Christian Williams	14	49	28.57%	59.20	0.57	64.29	1.86	1.49
Stuart Edmunds	12	37	32.43%	66.17	45.67	71.62	2.17	1.49
Neil Mulholland	12	44	27.27%	56.89	3.24	63.64	1.76	1.61
Dan Skelton	11	54	20.37%	58.86	-11.68	63.89	1.25	1.55
Neil King	11	80	13.75%	46.16	-6.83	58.75	0.87	1.03
Nicky Henderson	9	41	21.95%	61.95	-22.02	64.63	1.33	2.41
Paul Nicholls	8	32	25.00%	54.53	-9.37	57.81	1.20	1.75
Pam Sly	7	42	16.67%	64.31	6.88	73.81	1.12	1.37

FFOS LAS

Trainer	Wins	Runs	Strike Rate	% Rivals Beaten	P/L	Run To Form %	Impact Value	Market Value
Evan Williams	39	293	13.31%	51.13	-88.74	50.17	1.05	1.18
Peter Bowen	33	219	15.07%	50.28	-40.09	47.72	1.18	1.16
Nigel Twiston-Davies	22	114	19.30%	61.91	-9.66	62.28	1.58	1.68
David Rees	16	112	14.29%	51.16	33.13	44.64	1.24	1.13
Rebecca Curtis	16	79	20.25%	56.34	-7.25	56.33	1.67	1.50
Nicky Henderson	11	37	29.73%	62.61	-10.18	64.86	2.22	2.73
Tim Vaughan	11	130	8.46%	45.12	-35.50	46.54	0.67	0.98
Colin Tizzard	11	47	23.40%	55.80	24.23	56.38	1.93	1.60
Neil Mulholland	11	86	12.79%	52.48	1.25	58.14	1.04	1.02
David Pipe	10	78	12.82%	52.92	-47.43	55.77	1.08	1.71

FONTWELL PARK

Trainer	Wins	Runs	Strike Rate	% Rivals Beaten	P/L	Run To Form %	Impact Value	Market Value
Gary Moore	71	373	19.03%	56.01	-31.64	59.52	1.36	1.43
Neil Mulholland	37	203	18.23%	56.56	30.87	58.13	1.30	1.29
Paul Nicholls	37	98	37.76%	71.33	7.98	75.51	2.08	2.28
Chris Gordon	32	226	14.16%	53.58	-13.78	55.09	1.09	1.25
Anthony Honeyball	29	82	35.37%	68.52	23.44	69.51	2.35	2.16
Colin Tizzard	23	137	16.79%	52.71	-50.08	55.47	1.14	1.39
Philip Hobbs	20	76	26.32%	60.38	-15.97	65.79	1.85	2.18
Dan Skelton	17	95	17.89%	59.72	-33.11	61.58	1.19	1.61
Oliver Sherwood	16	93	17.20%	59.87	2.26	65.59	1.26	1.43
Alan King	16	56	28.57%	67.46	7.75	66.96	2.19	2.08

HAYDOCK PARK

Trainer	Wins	Runs	Strike Rate	% Rivals Beaten	P/L	Run To Form %	Impact Value	Market Value
Nigel Twiston-Davies	17	108	15.74%	54.58	-24.19	55.56	1.24	1.27
Sue Smith	15	93	16.13%	59.69	-14.75	61.83	1.20	1.29
Paul Nicholls	14	61	22.95%	56.84	-22.94	72.95	1.65	1.74
Nicky Henderson	14	50	28.00%	57.69	1.54	64.00	1.87	1.66
Donald McCain	13	95	13.68%	51.64	-34.22	55.79	0.95	0.98
Venetia Williams	12	63	19.05%	54.80	71.28	55.56	1.43	1.51
David Pipe	9	49	18.37%	55.97	13.58	56.12	1.80	1.52
Fergal O'Brien	8	32	25.00%	61.65	7.60	64.06	1.96	1.25
Jonjo O'Neill	7	35	20.00%	53.26	5.38	55.71	1.90	1.56
Evan Williams	6	66	9.09%	47.79	-33.75	44.70	0.68	1.15

HEREFORD

Trainer	Wins	Runs	Strike Rate	% Rivals Beaten	P/L	Run To Form %	Impact Value	Market Value
Dan Skelton	20	73	27.40%	62.50	0.50	65.07	2.20	2.23
Venetia Williams	19	100	19.00%	48.23	1.10	49.50	1.65	1.40
Nigel Twiston-Davies	11	51	21.57%	55.57	-9.97	56.86	1.73	1.67
Evan Williams	11	118	9.32%	46.33	-55.02	45.76	0.78	1.04
Kim Bailey	11	45	24.44%	64.50	2.43	67.78	2.14	1.88
Tom Symonds	10	50	20.00%	59.43	35.83	52.00	1.94	1.18
Philip Hobbs	10	47	21.28%	66.09	-18.85	76.60	1.68	2.19
Henry Oliver	9	68	13.24%	51.88	0.75	47.79	1.25	1.05
Nicky Henderson	8	18	44.44%	65.59	-1.47	66.67	3.48	3.21
Kerry Lee	8	60	13.33%	56.25	-23.55	59.17	1.06	1.34

HEXHAM

Trainer	Wins	Runs	Strike Rate	% Rivals Beaten	P/L	Run To Form %	Impact Value	Market Value
Lucinda Russell	32	234	13.68%	56.64	7.37	55.77	1.16	1.30
Micky Hammond	22	211	10.43%	47.01	-58.57	42.65	0.96	1.00
Maurice Barnes	18	156	11.54%	53.23	-54.00	51.92	1.00	1.06
Nicky Richards	15	49	30.61%	63.88	-3.15	62.24	2.61	2.68
Stuart Coltherd	15	102	14.71%	54.11	27.50	51.96	1.35	1.27
Mark Walford	11	77	14.29%	59.22	-10.85	58.44	1.32	1.42
Martin Todhunter	10	72	13.89%	57.40	-10.00	54.17	1.20	1.18
Ben Haslam	10	52	19.23%	50.50	29.30	50.00	1.52	1.17
James Ewart	10	66	15.15%	59.48	-14.00	53.79	1.46	1.48
Donald McCain	10	80	12.50%	52.37	-35.93	46.88	0.97	1.49

TRAINERS FOR COURSES

HUNTINGDON

Trainer	Wins	Runs	Strike Rate	% Rivals Beaten	P/L	Run To Form %	Impact Value	Market Value
Dan Skelton	30	155	19.35%	60.71	-45.06	60.65	1.64	2.03
Nicky Henderson	29	101	28.71%	67.71	-31.29	70.30	2.28	2.73
Jonjo O'Neill	20	116	17.24%	56.23	24.46	56.03	1.62	1.60
Kim Bailey	19	121	15.70%	53.12	-37.03	55.37	1.33	1.53
Fergal O'Brien	18	67	26.87%	59.59	53.96	62.69	2.23	1.75
Olly Murphy	14	52	26.92%	62.01	-9.15	66.35	2.27	1.73
Alan King	14	96	14.58%	65.96	-7.53	68.75	1.22	1.99
Gary Moore	13	112	11.61%	52.31	-20.00	50.00	1.01	1.32
Caroline Bailey	13	64	20.31%	57.74	24.46	54.69	1.81	1.08
Charlie Longsdon	11	107	10.28%	45.37	-30.25	49.53	0.92	0.99

KELSO

Trainer	Wins	Runs	Strike Rate	% Rivals Beaten	P/L	Run To Form %	Impact Value	Market Value
Lucinda Russell	32	271	11.81%	51.44	-80.51	49.63	0.96	1.02
Sandy Thomson	24	122	19.67%	59.45	56.98	64.75	1.46	1.38
N. W. Alexander	22	185	11.89%	47.58	46.26	49.46	0.96	1.01
Donald McCain	22	143	15.38%	54.65	-32.48	59.09	1.12	1.60
Keith Dalgleish	20	97	20.62%	57.01	18.22	58.25	1.64	1.81
Nicky Richards	19	112	16.96%	58.76	-10.85	60.71	1.21	1.72
Rose Dobbin	13	130	10.00%	55.13	-47.83	54.62	0.91	1.32
Iain Jardine	13	74	17.57%	57.05	-1.08	52.70	1.38	1.28
James Ewart	12	88	13.64%	50.73	11.88	51.14	1.09	1.19
Harriet Graham	10	73	13.70%	51.61	-26.67	55.48	1.05	0.92

KEMPTON PARK

Trainer	Wins	Runs	Strike Rate	% Rivals Beaten	P/L	Run To Form %	Impact Value	Market Value
Nicky Henderson	60	250	24.00%	60.09	-49.15	61.00	1.80	2.18
Paul Nicholls	56	251	22.31%	59.15	-24.35	65.54	1.53	1.75
Alan King	23	170	13.53%	54.04	-65.97	60.00	1.12	1.55
Dan Skelton	12	141	8.51%	48.92	-68.24	53.55	0.69	1.12
Nigel Twiston-Davies	12	88	13.64%	52.23	5.75	54.55	1.15	1.15
Harry Fry	12	60	20.00%	54.00	-6.13	50.83	1.70	1.51
Tom George	11	69	15.94%	56.13	3.75	70.29	1.25	1.26
Chris Gordon	11	87	12.64%	56.03	-38.40	55.75	1.12	1.25
Emma Lavelle	10	70	14.29%	55.72	107.70	57.86	1.16	1.18
Colin Tizzard	9	66	13.64%	56.45	42.85	56.82	1.16	1.16

LEICESTER

Trainer	Wins	Runs	Strike Rate	% Rivals Beaten	P/L	Run To Form %	Impact Value	Market Value
Dan Skelton	12	37	32.43%	65.15	2.42	68.92	2.19	1.78
Tom George	12	35	34.29%	69.44	15.87	72.86	2.34	1.64
Philip Hobbs	9	21	42.86%	74.75	12.25	76.19	2.85	2.18
Nigel Twiston-Davies	9	45	20.00%	60.85	8.11	65.56	1.35	1.35
Venetia Williams	9	35	25.71%	65.98	-4.13	67.14	1.71	2.26
Fergal O'Brien	8	40	20.00%	58.26	9.82	60.00	1.58	1.80
Caroline Bailey	7	32	21.88%	51.91	-0.47	54.69	1.49	1.29
Olly Murphy	6	19	31.58%	73.80	26.20	84.21	2.34	1.64
David Pipe	6	21	28.57%	60.44	-3.80	69.05	1.70	1.76
Gary Moore	6	26	23.08%	48.45	-2.08	46.15	1.73	1.62

LINGFIELD PARK

Trainer	Wins	Runs	Strike Rate	% Rivals Beaten	P/L	Run To Form %	Impact Value	Market Value
Gary Moore	19	133	14.29%	53.42	-21.47	54.89	1.12	1.28
Seamus Mullins	9	57	15.79%	51.40	81.38	44.74	1.37	0.78
Chris Gordon	9	49	18.37%	57.95	-13.03	53.06	1.39	1.36
Nicky Henderson	8	30	26.67%	66.89	-6.64	66.67	2.36	2.72
Nigel Twiston-Davies	5	48	10.42%	64.20	-17.25	54.17	1.01	1.62
Lucy Wadham	5	27	18.52%	63.58	25.94	55.56	1.61	1.31
Emma Lavelle	5	20	25.00%	66.02	6.50	62.50	2.26	1.66
Dan Skelton	5	31	16.13%	62.47	-14.40	53.23	1.33	2.28
Jamie Snowden	5	26	19.23%	62.56	-5.46	57.69	1.60	1.81
Ian Williams	5	14	35.71%	76.08	29.16	78.57	3.50	2.29

LUDLOW

Trainer	Wins	Runs	Strike Rate	% Rivals Beaten	P/L	Run To Form %	Impact Value	Market Value
Nicky Henderson	30	108	27.78%	62.85	-8.07	69.44	2.15	2.39
Dan Skelton	27	126	21.43%	62.99	-42.93	61.51	1.72	2.19
Henry Daly	23	105	21.90%	58.72	-13.62	59.05	1.84	1.44
Philip Hobbs	22	107	20.56%	63.10	-5.65	65.89	1.61	1.87
Nigel Twiston-Davies	20	141	14.18%	54.11	-51.45	54.26	1.18	1.43
Kim Bailey	20	101	19.80%	57.16	-9.00	61.39	1.67	1.85
Paul Nicholls	19	70	27.14%	60.53	-11.95	65.00	1.69	2.11
Venetia Williams	16	89	17.98%	60.19	-6.30	63.48	1.56	1.38
Evan Williams	15	180	8.33%	48.17	-106.88	49.72	0.64	1.11
Alan King	14	54	25.93%	67.01	-2.70	74.07	1.90	2.03

TRAINERS FOR COURSES

MARKET RASEN

Trainer	Wins	Runs	Strike Rate	% Rivals Beaten	P/L	Run To Form %	Impact Value	Market Value
Dan Skelton	58	254	22.83%	61.46	-27.12	62.60	1.74	1.96
Olly Murphy	37	184	20.11%	61.57	-43.85	62.23	1.60	1.70
Fergal O'Brien	26	137	18.98%	56.37	-12.22	63.14	1.43	1.63
Dr Richard Newland	22	79	27.85%	63.59	15.36	66.46	2.26	2.05
Nicky Henderson	22	75	29.33%	64.02	-11.18	68.67	2.14	2.29
Jonjo O'Neill	20	136	14.71%	51.24	-24.60	55.15	1.17	1.35
Alan King	18	100	18.00%	59.71	-15.43	64.00	1.43	1.59
Brian Ellison	14	93	15.05%	50.11	-20.13	55.38	1.18	1.34
Nigel Twiston-Davies	14	84	16.67%	51.78	4.85	54.76	1.40	1.58
Peter Bowen	13	83	15.66%	50.25	-2.33	58.43	1.35	1.34

MUSSELBURGH

Trainer	Wins	Runs	Strike Rate	% Rivals Beaten	P/L	Run To Form %	Impact Value	Market Value
Keith Dalgleish	34	156	21.79%	56.91	-5.93	60.26	1.72	1.53
Donald McCain	31	150	20.67%	61.51	37.12	64.00	1.53	1.48
Lucinda Russell	28	266	10.53%	48.51	-70.68	48.31	0.83	0.98
Paul Nicholls	21	49	42.86%	68.41	19.78	74.49	2.91	2.38
Sandy Thomson	17	87	19.54%	58.40	-0.87	62.07	1.51	1.53
N. W. Alexander	11	87	12.64%	56.75	-25.25	53.45	1.11	1.19
Iain Jardine	10	128	7.81%	53.01	-53.56	52.73	0.63	1.10
Rose Dobbin	8	56	14.29%	56.35	-13.75	65.18	1.27	1.27
Jim Goldie	8	86	9.30%	48.60	-9.75	43.60	0.81	0.91
Nicky Richards	8	65	12.31%	51.79	-6.50	49.23	1.11	1.56

NEWBURY

Trainer	Wins	Runs	Strike Rate	% Rivals Beaten	P/L	Run To Form %	Impact Value	Market Value
Nicky Henderson	59	242	24.38%	62.06	8.08	68.39	2.32	2.24
Paul Nicholls	30	152	19.74%	57.29	25.58	63.49	1.59	1.56
Philip Hobbs	25	131	19.08%	59.33	65.62	65.65	1.71	1.48
Colin Tizzard	18	127	14.17%	54.61	-41.31	55.12	1.21	1.43
Alan King	15	172	8.72%	58.61	-99.07	66.57	0.84	1.39
Ben Pauling	10	74	13.51%	51.80	-17.50	53.38	1.36	1.38
Dan Skelton	10	125	8.00%	50.08	-58.52	53.60	0.77	1.25
David Pipe	9	47	19.15%	59.56	16.33	65.96	2.17	1.27
Harry Fry	7	53	13.21%	48.65	-16.92	54.72	1.43	2.25
Jonjo O'Neill	7	71	9.86%	47.89	-13.50	48.59	1.09	1.18

NEWCASTLE

Trainer	Wins	Runs	Strike Rate	% Rivals Beaten	P/L	Run To Form %	Impact Value	Market Value
Sue Smith	22	106	20.75%	62.46	12.86	65.57	1.67	1.57
Brian Ellison	17	91	18.68%	59.74	-38.52	59.89	1.44	1.71
Nicky Richards	14	87	16.09%	54.18	-20.31	52.30	1.24	1.78
Micky Hammond	14	118	11.86%	45.95	-36.48	42.80	0.96	0.97
Rebecca Menzies	13	94	13.83%	55.36	-1.42	48.40	1.16	1.18
Sandy Thomson	13	64	20.31%	60.59	91.13	67.19	1.48	1.58
Philip Kirby	13	110	11.82%	50.45	-33.58	47.73	1.02	1.12
James Ewart	12	83	14.46%	51.60	-18.50	45.78	1.12	1.29
Lucinda Russell	10	102	9.80%	47.55	-43.63	43.14	0.80	0.96
Keith Dalgleish	10	47	21.28%	59.80	30.10	55.32	1.79	1.75

NEWTON ABBOT

Trainer	Wins	Runs	Strike Rate	% Rivals Beaten	P/L	Run To Form %	Impact Value	Market Value
Paul Nicholls	41	148	27.70%	63.78	-48.90	65.54	1.59	2.20
Colin Tizzard	30	168	17.86%	57.21	-7.00	58.04	1.26	1.37
Philip Hobbs	20	134	14.93%	55.63	-55.14	60.82	1.15	1.70
Fergal O'Brien	19	72	26.39%	68.74	16.50	69.44	2.29	1.95
Jeremy Scott	13	83	15.66%	53.81	-16.75	48.80	1.33	1.23
David Pipe	13	132	9.85%	48.90	-47.67	51.14	0.80	1.30
Evan Williams	12	93	12.90%	53.69	-32.65	53.76	0.90	1.23
Peter Bowen	12	63	19.05%	55.54	31.31	57.14	1.45	1.25
Emma Lavelle	12	49	24.49%	57.33	31.75	62.24	1.88	1.35
Nicky Henderson	12	33	36.36%	63.12	7.96	75.76	2.37	2.08

PERTH

Trainer	Wins	Runs	Strike Rate	% Rivals Beaten	P/L	Run To Form %	Impact Value	Market Value
Gordon Elliott, Ireland	55	209	26.32%	65.26	-46.62	68.18	1.78	2.06
Lucinda Russell	32	345	9.28%	47.30	-86.72	44.78	0.73	0.92
Fergal O'Brien	22	79	27.85%	61.14	15.37	64.56	1.96	1.80
Nicky Richards	17	154	11.04%	54.61	-49.67	59.09	0.88	1.45
Donald McCain	17	66	25.76%	54.66	13.73	64.39	1.71	1.21
Nigel Twiston-Davies	14	76	18.42%	55.92	-32.66	57.24	1.30	1.83
Keith Dalgleish	14	63	22.22%	55.44	2.24	62.70	1.60	1.48
Peter Bowen	12	31	38.71%	68.48	16.37	69.35	2.73	1.93
Lisa Harrison	11	118	9.32%	40.54	-34.92	41.10	0.72	0.84
Neil Mulholland	10	45	22.22%	64.08	11.63	67.78	1.75	1.71

PLUMPTON

Trainer	Wins	Runs	Strike Rate	% Rivals Beaten	P/L	Run To Form %	Impact Value	Market Value
Gary Moore	53	351	15.10%	52.44	-85.33	56.27	1.09	1.48
Chris Gordon	38	178	21.35%	59.85	0.68	63.76	1.61	1.53
Anthony Honeyball	18	72	25.00%	56.39	-9.41	65.28	1.73	1.99
Seamus Mullins	15	117	12.82%	50.25	-7.59	45.73	0.96	1.00
Paul Nicholls	14	32	43.75%	67.23	19.69	68.75	2.54	2.25
Sheena West	13	86	15.12%	53.16	44.25	49.42	1.29	1.03
Neil Mulholland	13	115	11.30%	51.53	-60.13	48.26	0.88	1.17
Neil King	13	65	20.00%	53.16	-20.01	53.08	1.28	1.32
Dan Skelton	12	44	27.27%	64.65	-16.00	64.77	2.10	2.50
Alan King	12	46	26.09%	65.62	-12.04	76.09	1.82	2.34

SANDOWN PARK

Trainer	Wins	Runs	Strike Rate	% Rivals Beaten	P/L	Run To Form %	Impact Value	Market Value
Nicky Henderson	37	148	25.00%	59.87	-19.20	61.82	2.00	2.03
Gary Moore	18	160	11.25%	45.74	-82.38	48.75	0.88	0.99
Paul Nicholls	17	153	11.11%	53.01	-60.30	65.36	0.85	1.30
Philip Hobbs	15	88	17.05%	57.72	-6.40	58.52	1.50	1.47
Nigel Twiston-Davies	12	60	20.00%	52.38	66.80	55.00	1.91	1.37
Colin Tizzard	11	85	12.94%	47.62	-39.70	54.71	1.10	1.34
Fergal O'Brien	10	45	22.22%	56.38	19.00	60.00	1.99	1.37
Venetia Williams	10	73	13.70%	52.21	-14.88	55.48	1.20	1.36
Alan King	9	51	17.65%	61.11	5.13	74.51	1.43	1.56
David Pipe	7	42	16.67%	50.50	-3.04	46.43	1.65	1.41

SEDGEFIELD

Trainer	Wins	Runs	Strike Rate	% Rivals Beaten	P/L	Run To Form %	Impact Value	Market Value
Donald McCain	37	253	14.62%	57.41	-25.57	58.89	1.04	1.42
Brian Ellison	37	146	25.34%	60.96	-10.23	64.04	1.71	1.59
Micky Hammond	27	286	9.44%	43.85	-139.02	38.99	0.74	0.94
Sue Smith	26	145	17.93%	56.77	-14.75	57.24	1.37	1.39
Sam England	21	104	20.19%	55.84	13.15	55.29	1.54	1.29
Neil Mulholland	18	49	36.73%	62.86	3.09	68.37	2.41	2.15
Philip Kirby	18	116	15.52%	53.05	6.58	48.28	1.30	1.23
Rebecca Menzies	17	122	13.93%	54.82	4.57	56.15	1.11	1.04
Dianne Sayer	17	82	20.73%	55.36	45.46	53.05	1.82	1.28
Evan Williams	16	53	30.19%	62.52	22.54	63.21	2.03	1.62

SOUTHWELL

Trainer	Wins	Runs	Strike Rate	% Rivals Beaten	P/L	Run To Form %	Impact Value	Market Value
Dan Skelton	50	227	22.03%	63.24	-59.16	67.84	1.74	2.14
Nicky Henderson	24	63	38.10%	68.67	5.80	73.02	2.63	2.50
Jonjo O'Neill	21	150	14.00%	56.59	-45.55	54.67	1.14	1.44
Olly Murphy	17	99	17.17%	57.80	-52.59	57.58	1.45	1.85
Fergal O'Brien	16	76	21.05%	57.39	8.82	55.92	1.86	1.76
Tom George	15	81	18.52%	63.90	-26.96	68.52	1.37	1.77
Harry Whittington	14	53	26.42%	66.43	47.86	67.92	2.31	1.72
Alan King	14	51	27.45%	70.26	-2.53	70.59	1.84	2.00
Caroline Bailey	14	84	16.67%	57.16	-17.50	53.57	1.38	1.48
Dr Richard Newland	14	56	25.00%	67.25	-17.68	68.75	1.96	2.22

STRATFORD-ON-AVON

Trainer	Wins	Runs	Strike Rate	% Rivals Beaten	P/L	Run To Form %	Impact Value	Market Value
Dan Skelton	35	165	21.21%	61.14	-46.38	63.94	1.64	2.09
Dr Richard Newland	17	60	28.33%	63.45	-20.52	64.17	1.94	2.18
Nigel Twiston-Davies	15	82	18.29%	56.99	-19.34	55.49	1.39	1.53
Donald McCain	15	65	23.08%	62.68	28.00	55.38	1.70	1.31
Olly Murphy	14	103	13.59%	49.35	-55.38	51.46	1.11	1.53
Tom George	14	74	18.92%	56.56	-4.87	57.43	1.49	1.81
Neil Mulholland	13	79	16.46%	54.82	18.58	55.06	1.26	1.18
Paul Nicholls	13	34	38.24%	73.37	3.84	77.94	2.71	2.65
Charlie Longsdon	13	70	18.57%	59.28	4.03	65.71	1.47	1.28
Fergal O'Brien	13	79	16.46%	58.50	-13.72	56.96	1.31	1.85

TAUNTON

Trainer	Wins	Runs	Strike Rate	% Rivals Beaten	P/L	Run To Form %	Impact Value	Market Value
Paul Nicholls	51	192	26.56%	69.48	-20.25	69.27	2.13	2.67
Philip Hobbs	24	150	16.00%	63.30	-38.38	68.00	1.48	1.60
Colin Tizzard	18	136	13.24%	49.74	-8.60	45.59	1.18	1.35
Harry Fry	18	82	21.95%	60.30	-20.20	64.63	1.94	2.17
Jeremy Scott	15	76	19.74%	61.26	34.48	61.18	1.93	1.63
Neil Mulholland	13	106	12.26%	50.65	-14.42	41.98	1.21	1.15
David Pipe	12	139	8.63%	51.01	-64.56	44.60	0.83	1.26
Nicky Henderson	12	38	31.58%	73.90	3.71	78.95	2.46	2.22
Evan Williams	10	123	8.13%	48.64	-70.63	43.09	0.70	0.99
Dan Skelton	9	73	12.33%	50.00	-44.05	58.22	1.10	1.60

TRAINERS FOR COURSES

UTTOXETER

Trainer	Wins	Runs	Strike Rate	% Rivals Beaten	P/L	Run To Form %	Impact Value	Market Value
Dan Skelton	85	304	27.96%	65.70	29.16	64.47	2.50	2.25
Jonjo O'Neill	31	236	13.14%	49.01	-48.20	48.52	1.22	1.40
Dr Richard Newland	26	95	27.37%	66.94	2.09	65.79	2.25	2.20
Nicky Henderson	25	87	28.74%	62.95	-8.63	59.77	2.21	2.34
Harry Fry	21	77	27.27%	57.01	13.75	63.64	2.36	2.04
Fergal O'Brien	20	120	16.67%	59.88	20.18	62.92	1.45	1.66
Charlie Longsdon	19	119	15.97%	53.91	-1.38	56.30	1.47	1.36
Neil Mulholland	18	143	12.59%	50.44	-23.12	50.00	1.19	1.26
Olly Murphy	18	91	19.78%	60.83	0.29	58.24	1.72	1.77
Nigel Twiston-Davies	18	145	12.41%	55.66	-68.15	55.52	1.16	1.52

WARWICK

Trainer	Wins	Runs	Strike Rate	% Rivals Beaten	P/L	Run To Form %	Impact Value	Market Value
Dan Skelton	85	304	27.96%	65.70	29.16	64.47	2.50	2.25
Jonjo O'Neill	31	236	13.14%	49.01	-48.20	48.52	1.22	1.40
Dr Richard Newland	26	95	27.37%	66.94	2.09	65.79	2.25	2.20
Nicky Henderson	25	87	28.74%	62.95	-8.63	59.77	2.21	2.34
Harry Fry	21	77	27.27%	57.01	13.75	63.64	2.36	2.04
Fergal O'Brien	20	120	16.67%	59.88	20.18	62.92	1.45	1.66
Charlie Longsdon	19	119	15.97%	53.91	-1.38	56.30	1.47	1.36
Neil Mulholland	18	143	12.59%	50.44	-23.12	50.00	1.19	1.26
Olly Murphy	18	91	19.78%	60.83	0.29	58.24	1.72	1.77
Nigel Twiston-Davies	18	145	12.41%	55.66	-68.15	55.52	1.16	1.52

WETHERBY

Trainer	Wins	Runs	Strike Rate	% Rivals Beaten	P/L	Run To Form %	Impact Value	Market Value
Dan Skelton	43	159	27.04%	66.20	-0.20	70.44	2.10	2.05
Philip Kirby	25	197	12.69%	46.35	-24.38	45.94	1.18	0.91
Micky Hammond	19	293	6.48%	44.34	-46.50	42.32	0.59	0.69
Nigel Twiston-Davies	14	77	18.18%	55.71	-22.92	61.04	1.37	1.73
Sue Smith	12	168	7.14%	50.09	-115.06	52.08	0.59	1.19
Kim Bailey	12	55	21.82%	64.11	-11.63	66.36	1.69	2.10
Fergal O'Brien	11	40	27.50%	63.61	6.09	62.50	2.45	2.69
Brian Ellison	11	82	13.41%	56.52	-30.95	62.80	0.97	1.21
Nicky Richards	11	51	21.57%	55.41	33.75	60.78	1.69	1.46
Jonjo O'Neill	11	80	13.75%	55.75	-36.36	60.00	1.21	1.49

WINCANTON

Trainer	Wins	Runs	Strike Rate	% Rivals Beaten	P/L	Run To Form %	Impact Value	Market Value
Paul Nicholls	101	307	32.90%	67.28	5.10	71.99	2.33	2.67
Colin Tizzard	36	285	12.63%	56.19	-69.13	55.96	1.09	1.40
Philip Hobbs	19	177	10.73%	55.42	-41.21	58.19	0.99	1.33
Neil Mulholland	18	163	11.04%	55.27	-7.05	52.15	0.93	1.09
Jeremy Scott	15	126	11.90%	52.82	-22.33	53.57	1.07	1.19
Harry Fry	15	92	16.30%	54.85	-8.31	54.89	1.43	1.81
Emma Lavelle	12	67	17.91%	61.19	12.84	62.69	1.71	1.61
Alan King	11	79	13.92%	59.04	-41.63	62.66	1.20	1.71
Robert Walford	9	76	11.84%	49.23	-17.25	37.50	1.12	1.05
Chris Gordon	9	37	24.32%	58.43	58.00	60.81	2.33	1.18

WORCESTER

Trainer	Wins	Runs	Strike Rate	% Rivals Beaten	P/L	Run To Form %	Impact Value	Market Value
Philip Hobbs	28	97	28.87%	62.30	70.23	59.79	2.28	1.90
Dan Skelton	28	162	17.28%	58.31	-38.97	57.41	1.37	1.88
Dr Richard Newland	24	81	29.63%	68.42	0.35	74.07	2.23	2.14
Jonjo O'Neill	22	164	13.41%	54.12	-59.18	57.01	1.10	1.39
Peter Bowen	20	101	19.80%	59.34	51.55	62.87	1.67	1.49
David Pipe	18	107	16.82%	57.81	33.00	64.95	1.49	1.34
Nicky Henderson	18	77	23.38%	63.18	-13.08	68.18	1.75	2.18
Neil Mulholland	17	149	11.41%	51.37	-64.97	52.01	0.95	1.22
Nigel Twiston-Davies	16	75	21.33%	59.17	-8.88	61.33	1.78	1.45
Alan King	14	57	24.56%	69.09	-11.80	70.18	2.12	2.12

Index

Index To Photographers